CHILDREN
OF THE DUST

An Okie Family Story

BETTY GRANT HENSHAW

EDITED BY SANDRA SCOFIELD

INTRODUCTION BY VICTORIA SMITH

TEXAS TECH UNIVERSITY PRESS

This book is typeset in Sabon. The paper used in this book meets the minimum
requirements of ANSI/NISO Z39.48-1992 (R1997). ∞

Designed by David Timmons

Library of Congress Cataloging-in-Publication Data
Henshaw, Betty Grant, 1933–
    Children of the dust : an Okie family story / Betty Grant Henshaw ; edited by
Sandra Scofield ; introduction by Victoria Smith.
        p.   cm.
    Summary: "Dust Bowl memoir of a family who held on tenant-farming in
Oklahoma years after their relatives westered to California. Focuses on Hen-
shaw's father, who would not leave until he could pay his way to California, and
on her parents' strong marriage and how it sustained the family of eleven"—Pro-
vided by the publisher.
    Includes bibliographical references and index.
    ISBN-13: 978-0-89672-631-4 (pbk : alk. paper)
    ISBN-10: 0-89672-631-2 (pbk : alk. paper) 1. Grant family. 2. Henshaw,
Betty Grant, 1933—Childhood and youth. 3. Tenant farmers—Oklahoma—
Biography. 4. Dust Bowl Era, 1931–1939. 5. Oklahoma—Biography. 6. California—Biography. I. Scofield, Sandra Jean, 1943– II. Title. III. Series.
    CT274.G68H46 2006
    976.6'053—dc22
                                    2006005172
First paperback printing, 2008

Printed in the United States of America
08 09 10 11 12 13 14 15 16 / 9 8 7 6 5 4 3 2 1

Texas Tech University Press
Box 41037
Lubbock, Texas 79409-1037 USA
800.832.4042
ttup@ttu.edu
www.ttup.ttu.edu

PLAINS HISTORIES

John R. Wunder, Series Editor

CHILDREN OF THE DUST

To Mama and Daddy.
And to my siblings: Helen, the baby sister we never knew,
Robert, Tink, Sid, Judy and June, Susie, Kitty, and Jimmy,
without whom there would be no story.

Contents

CALIFORNIA

Preface

SANDRA SCOFIELD

MY GRANDMOTHER'S FAMILY came to Oklahoma Territory when it opened to white settlement, and my grandmother was born in Ada. Her grandparents and parents were farmers, though her father died when she was young. She and her husband tried to farm, too, but the drought and poverty of the thirties drove them from the land. After my grandfather's untimely death, my grandmother worked for the railroad, and, ultimately, General Mills. I spent many days of my childhood with her at her stepfather's farm in Devol, where, without irrigation or even running water in the house, he and my great-grandmother would toil until their late seventies.

I say this to explain why I have always been fascinated by the narratives of the Dust Bowl. Somehow the hardships and sorrows of those times came to represent part of the myth of my family for me: failed hopes and dreams, forced exile, fractured relationships. In the end, all the farm experience meant for me, personally, was visiting a home that still had an outhouse, eating fresh chicken, and sometimes, when they forgot I was near, hearing the women remember their lost loved ones.

So when Betty Henshaw approached me and said that she had stories about her family's farming life in Oklahoma, I was interested, and when I heard her tell some of them, I was enthralled. She has a stature that bespeaks her stubbornness, her resilience, and at the same time, her humility. I warmed to her as one might to someone introduced by kin. At that time, she was still learning to construct a narrative, and over the years, I spoke with her now and then, glad to hear that she had the support of friends and classes. She was going to write her family stories, and she was going to do it right. "Right" became a manuscript with the immediacy and warmth of an oral history.

What I wasn't prepared for was a manuscript that made me so happy to read: not another Dust Bowl story, not a tale of failure, but a story with a strong family and a good life. Her father was truly a man of the land, and he loved it and worked it until he was old. He was also a religious man, who kept a short leash on his children but always, always out of love and high expectations, and he was charitable and trustworthy to everyone. The marriage of Betty's parents was a model of cooperation and mutual respect, and within it the children grew up happy, competent, and responsible.

To read such a story is a pleasure. To discover in it a wealth of fresh details about life in small towns and on farms of the period from the late thirties into the fifties is a treasure. The Grants loved each other and their lives, and it fell to Betty by her nature to record that loving world, with its struggles and its abundant fun, its good folk, and above all, a family that flourished, even in hard times.

Missoula, Montana, 2006

Introduction

Victoria Smith

NOT MUCH EVER CHANGES in Oklahoma. Morbid aridity and her offspring—drought, dust, and fire—have characterized life there ever since the abrupt intrusion of white American settlers in the infamous land rush of 1889.

Originally the homeland of the Kiowa and Kiowa-Apache Indians, Oklahoma's indigenous population swelled from the 1820s through the 1840s when almost twenty thousand Native Americans were forced west of the Mississippi River under the federal removal policy. The most commemorated of these removals was the Cherokees' Trail of Tears, but their removal from lands east of the Mississippi was by no means singular. Most of the forcibly removed Indians, like the Cherokees, made Oklahoma their new home, but in the wake of their passing they left stragglers, strays, and runaways in the Missouri and Arkansas Ozarks. Other Cherokees, generally called Old Settlers because they were early migrants to the Ozarks, lived there as well. It was among these Ozark Cherokees that Betty Grant Henshaw's mother, Elsie Burton Bristol, was born, and their home is where Betty's memoir, *Children of the Dust,* begins. Like other Okie memoirs before hers, Betty's story recalls a close-knit family, the strain of the Dust Bowl years, and the family's relocation to California. But memories of her teenage years toiling in the fields of the "promised land" make this story uniquely her own.

White intruders slaughtered the last of the buffalo in Oklahoma in the 1870s. Beginning in 1889 and continuing through the 1930s, the delicate ecological balance of Oklahoma fell victim to the onslaught of the "Boomers" and "Sooners" and their capitalist agricultural practices. Hundreds of thousands of acres of Oklahoma sod felt the rip of the plow and the heavy hooves of countless Missouri mules, indelibly violating the old Indian Territory's virgin soil. Just as many acres found their vegetation sheared to the ground by grazing cattle. The stock market collapse of 1929 fell especially hard across the Great Plains, compounding Oklahoma's misery. The combined depression and drought blew an impenetrable cloud of dust and poverty southward across the state.[1]

Even as this introduction is written, wildfires are devouring thousands of acres of an especially parched Oklahoma and are threatening to consume more; burnt-out homes and charred dreams are left in their path. Given the long-standing challenges of surviving in Oklahoma, it is not surprising that the red-earth state has produced some of the most popular American literature ever written. The most recent contribution, Betty Grant Henshaw's *Children of the Dust,* adds an important and unique perspective to the well-established genre of Oklahoma memoirs.

Henshaw is a native of Oklahoma, as is Cherokee poet and playwright Lynn Riggs. Betty was born near Hominy, north of Claremore, in 1933. During her lifetime, Betty's father would resist increasing pressure to abandon the Oklahoma farmland for California, but he eventually capitulated in the 1940s—against his better judgment but to the initial delight of his family. Rollo Lynn Riggs, whose stage play *Green Grow the Lilacs* would eventually be immortalized as the stage and screen production *Oklahoma!,* was a prolific writer whose achievements include numerous plays, a prestigious Guggenheim award, world-wide travel, and membership in the *avante* artistic guard that grew up with Santa Fe in the 1920s. And although *Green Grow the Lilacs* would prove to be Riggs's most popular and enduring work, two of his other plays come closer to capturing the Oklahoma of Betty Grant Henshaw's childhood.[2]

The first, *Sump'n Like Wings* (1928), which Riggs described as "my first serious long play" was based on "people I had known in Oklahoma." The story rotates around an impoverished young girl named Willie, who resolves to rise above her peculiarly Oklahoman brand of poverty. Like Willie, the Grant family struggled for self-reliance in the parched earth of eastern Oklahoma. They retained a sense of dignity and self-respect despite the poverty that bound them to the worthless soil. The Grants learned to rely on close family ties, neighbors, and community, and, like Willie, they learned to fly on *Sump'n Like Wings.*[3]

The second Riggs play speaks to the Indian heritage that colors Oklahoma's cultural history and the Grant family background. *The Cherokee Night* (1931) was Riggs's personal favorite. In it, he turns a dramatic eye to "the descendants of the Cherokee Indians in Oklahoma." He wrote to a friend that the idea had come from a traditional Cherokee saying:

> The grass is withered;
> Where the river was is red sand;
> Fire eats the timber-Night has come to our people.

The play, he continued, "will concern itself with that night, that darkness . . . which has come to the Cherokees and their descendants. An absorbed race has its curiously irreconcilable inheritance. It seems to me that the best grade of absorbed Indian might be an intellectual Hamlet, buffeted, harassed, victimized, split, baffled—with somewhere in him great fire and some granite . . ."[4]

Like Riggs, whose mother was one-eighth Cherokee, Betty Grant Henshaw was born to people that can affectionately be termed "sump'n like Indians." As do many Oklahomans, the Grant family traced their ancestry to the Cherokees but found themselves caught, along with many other descendants, in the machinations of American imperialism, stripped of all legal Indian identity. Yet, just as Riggs had perceived, the Grants would prove to be made of fire and granite.[5]

Vestiges of an Indian heritage lingered in the Grant family. Most obviously, it can be found in the presence of the extended family clan so typical of Cherokees, even today. It can also be seen in the idealization of male clan heads—in Betty's case, her dirt-bitten, tenant-farmer father, Bill Grant—that would signal the waning of matrilineal clans. While most American settlers struck out for the West individually or as small, nuclear families, Cherokees, like many Native Americans, clung to their blood relations and frequently migrated together. Although Americanization, particularly Christianity, mowed down the Cherokees' traditional social organization, and patriarchy eventually replaced matriarchy as the central focus of Cherokee clan organization, the clan formation itself survived, as evidenced by *Children of the Dust.* Coaxed by extended family members who had already migrated to California, Bill Grant would reluctantly follow suit with his family, certain that better days in Oklahoma lay just one more harvest away but unwilling to ask his long-suffering family to try their Okalahoma luck once again.

"I don't remember when it began," Betty recalled of her childhood, "but as far back as my mind can reach, Mama and Daddy talked about leaving the farm in Oklahoma and moving to California. Each year as the crops were gathered in, Mama's dreams were shattered as Daddy decided to stay and farm one more year."

But Bill Grant wasn't the only stubborn man in Oklahoma. Indeed, Oklahoma literature is filled with rugged characters dating back to the Indian Territory days; men like Cherokee Achilles Smith, whose outlawry led to his infamous hanging. With the passing of Indian Territory and the onset of Oklahoma statehood in 1907, a Cherokee named Will Rogers used his droll wit to bring tales of

Oklahoma's frontier characters to life in Wild West shows, in the Ziegfeld follies, and in radio. Rogers also entertained readers with hundreds of newspaper columns, articles, and books rooted in the characters he had grown up amongst in the old Cherokee Nation, and, eventually, he made his appearance in film. "During the bleak years of the Great Depression," wrote one essayist, "he came to represent the common person, the casual humorist and raconteur, the man who clung to the folkways of a mythical nineteenth-century American west that seemed so long ago."[6]

Will Rogers's performances created a market for a plethora of memoirs revolving around other larger-than-life men. For example, *Hands Up! Stories of the Six-Gun Fighters of the Old Wild West* as told by Fred E. Sutton and recorded by A. B. McDonald in 1927, begins predictably enough.

> On the thirty-sixth anniversary of the opening of Oklahoma to white settlement there was a great street parade in Oklahoma City. . . . Leading the parade, on horseback, with their old saddles and six-shooters, was a group of men, grizzled veterans of the days when all that was buffalo land, when it was all wild country, when land and grass were free, when only the venturesome and brave dared forth upon the plains; when the six-shooter was the arbiter in almost all serious disputes; men who had entered Oklahoma in the greatest horse race ever run, in which the prize was a homestead; and among those men, at the head of the parade, was Fred E. Sutton.[7]

Paul McClung's *Papa Jack: Cowman from the Wichitas* (1975), the story of an Oklahoma pioneer, perpetuated the genre. "It was not that [Papa Jack] was a person who never grew up," wrote McClung. "He had grown wise in his growing. It was that he managed to retain a child's outlandish capacity to play and to learn. Papa Jack's recipe for trouble was grit your teeth and grow through it."[8]

Most recently, Robert K. DeArment's *Alias Frank Canton* traces the life of a deputy marshal in Oklahoma Territory who took on the slippery Doolin-Dalton gang. Although he had never before been a lawman, Canton relished the appointment. "I went to Oklahoma in the Spring of 1894 [and] decided to again enter the service of the U.S. and the Ter. of Okla. as a field officer to assist in hunting down the Outlaw bands who openly defied the laws of the Country," begins his Oklahoma narrative.[9]

But it would take John Steinbeck to realize that the desperados of days gone by had been transformed by drought and poverty into the desperate men of the great California migration. Men like Bill Grant would grudgingly pull up stake and head further west, where endless hours of labor and a mere pittance for wages would prove their granite core. The plight of impoverished Oklahoma farmers, regardless of race, set the stage for Steinbeck's classic tale of Oklahoma migrants, *The Grapes of Wrath* (1939).[10] Like Steinbeck's Joad family, Betty Grant Henshaw's people finally succumbed to the temptation of California, whose golden glow penetrated the grey skies of Oklahoma and lured away so many with promises of plentiful work. Like the Joads, the Grants became Steinbeck's *Harvest Gypsies*; inadvertently underscoring Geta Leseur's thesis that *Not All Okies Are White*. But the stark, harsh reality of life in the fields of California proved to be the foil to so many Okies' dreams, as it did for the *Children of the Dust*. Grant's descriptions of the migrants' children, particularly, illustrate California's deceptive cruelty.[11]

Betty painfully recalls a four-year-old boy named David who worked with his parents in the fields while his tiny sister babysat an even younger child: "The first time they went by, Mama said, 'Daddy, did you see that little boy's eyes? Looks like he can't hardly see.' We could see his eyes were almost glued shut from infection. He kept rubbing them and whining. He couldn't keep up with his parents, and his mother sent him back to the truck. . . ." The fate of the pitiful child is told in one of the most chilling passages in the book. Clearly, when contrasted with the harsh life of a migrant community, children old enough to remember Oklahoma would have had ample reason to fondly recall their childhood homes.

Indeed, beneath the chronicle of mixed-blood family history and Okie migrants, Grant's memoir is firmly rooted in an Oklahoma childhood, a story only she could tell, but one true to Oklahoma literature. "Now when I look back," Betty writes, "I'm thankful that Daddy waited [to migrate], because he gave me a rare and wonderful childhood in the Oklahoma hills. There were lessons I would only understand after my journey on Route 66, and the backbreaking work in the sun-baked California cotton fields. Now I see how the important parts of who I am spring from the rich experience of those early years, when I was the child of farmers, and a child of the land."

Other Oklahoma narratives, while often defined by the Dust Bowl days, poignantly recall growing up in Oklahoma despite the odds. David G. Siceloff's *Boy Settler in the Cherokee Strip* (1964) was among the first of these recollections. Siceloff described the Oklahoma wind as it scoured the prairie floor: "The days slipped together and the hot winds blew. Heat danced everywhere and whirlwinds whipped the dust and tumbleweeds high in the air until they seemed as high as the buzzards that were always circling and looking for some animal carcasses."[12] But despite the sparse landscape, Siceloff would fondly remember his childhood decades after leaving the old homestead. Central to his thoughts was that mainstay of Oklahoma narratives, the idealized male. In the final passage of his book Siceloff wrote, "It was many years before I saw the claim again. The buildings were all gone and the wells filled up. . . . I was asked to clear up the mystery of a mound two miles west on the county line. . . . It was all that was left of Olmsteads' sod house where father, wet and muddy, had taken refuge from the storm the night he walked nine miles to save fifty cents." Stubborn men, those Oklahomans, and keenly remembered for it.[13]

More recently, in *Five Shades of Shadow* (2003), Tracy Daugherty has written of his childhood in West Texas and southern Oklahoma. He originally intended to write "an old-fashioned, unironic story about the economic hope socialism gave Oklahoma farmers just before the First World War" as it played out in his grandfather's lifetime. But "by the mid-1990s, not only was socialism long gone from American life (along with most family farmers) so was the straightforward, unironic storytelling I'd first discovered reading *The Grapes of Wrath*."[14]

Following the bombing of the Murrah building in downtown Oklahoma City—a "blast," Daughterty claimed, that sent him "whirling back to my childhood,"—and following the terror attack at the World Trade Center, Daugherty opted to write a work of "personal nonfiction" reflecting on his Oklahoma boyhood. Once again, as in *Children of the Dust,* an idealized male, Daugherty's grandfather, forms the center pivot of the narrative.[15] Daugherty nostalgically recalls the profound effect his grandfather had on his life.

> As a child, my grandfather displayed a precocious talent for public speaking. His dad taught him the socialist gospel, toured him by horse and buggy through Oklahoma and northern Texas and set him up on street-corner soapboxes to spread the Word. . . . He went on to a distinguished political career, serving twice in the Oklahoma House of Representatives. Throughout my childhood, I thrilled to see his name— *my* name—on campaign posters. . . . I didn't come from a family of readers. . . . Not until my grandfather gave me *The Grapes of Wrath* did I understand language's power to invoke the world, to illuminate the daily struggles of women and men.[16]

But in the end, it is with those who remember girlhood in Oklahoma that Betty Grant Henshaw's memoirs resonate most strongly, even when that memoir is fiction. Diane Glancy's 1998 novel, *Flutie,* cleverly anticipates Betty's stories of her childhood. In one scene, Flutie—like Betty, an Indian mixed-blood—has accompanied her mother to the secondhand store in Woodward, Oklahoma.

Flutie saw a dress. It was plaid. Made to wear in Heaven. For the Queen of Angels. "No," her mother said, but Flutie stood by the plaid dress with its short, puffy sleeves and white yoke and sash. . . . When her mother called her, Flutie still clung to the dress. She stood frozen when her mother walked to her. She cowered as if her mother would slap her, but her mother took the dress with Flutie attached to it and went to the front counter to pay. That's what Flutie would remember. Her legs trembling as the woman put the dress in a brown sack. Flutie held it to her chest as they drove off in the truck, her mother shifting awkwardly jerking Flutie's neck. . . . After the light was out that night, Flutie put on her dress and slept in it. . . . [She] waited for the school bus in her wrinkled dress, feeling the air on her legs. That's what dresses did to you. Let the air lick your knees.[17]

Contrast this with Betty's memory of shopping with her own mother in Holbrook, Arizona, on the way to California.

I followed [Mama] past a long glass window with a display of beautifully dressed mannequins. She opened the door and we stepped inside. . . . Someone said, "Can I help you?" Mama said, "I'm looking for her a coat," nodding toward me. The clerk led us across the store to a round rack of new winter coats. Mama shuffled past everything until she found

a deep red. [She] said to me, "Slip your arms in here." I
wrapped the coat around me. It was warm and soft. . . . It
was Mama who loved red, so when she asked me if I liked it,
I said I did. . . . She turned to the clerk and said, "We'll take
it." . . . Then Daddy said, "Let's go. I want to get to Flagstaff
before it's too late." Mama tucked my coat away carefully
behind the seat, where it wouldn't get dirty.

Moreover, LaVerne Hanners recalled the complicated relation-
ship between women, clothing, and Oklahoma in her 1994 memoir,
Girl on a Pony. Hanners's family lived on a rise in the southern plains
known as Black Mesa—the tallest point in Oklahoma, marking the
spot where the grasslands of western Oklahoma flow into those of
New Mexico and Colorado, a no-man's land as remote today as it
was in Hanners's childhood. Like Betty Grant's mother, LaVerne
Hanners's mother was an accomplished seamstress, able to fashion
finery out of flour sacks with ease. One day, rare company came calling, and Laverne was determined to show off her mother's skill.

I remember one dress Mother had before Dad died. It was
plum-colored satin with a bodice of gold brigade. . . . I
thought the dress and hat were the most beautiful things I
had ever seen, and they probably were. . . . There was important company at the ranch. . . . The men brought their wives
along, and they were beautifully dressed. I was determined
that they should see my mother had a dress every bit as fine
as theirs. . . . I came back down the landing and, leaning out,
gently waved that dress like a banner. . . . There was a stifled
giggle or two and then Mother said, "LaVerne, why don't
you show the ladies the jacket. It's really the nicest part of
the dress." The ladies were gracious and made nice com-
ments. I am to this day almost overcome with gratitude that
Mother didn't fail me.[18]

Clearly, despite poverty and isolation, clothing was a mechanism of communication in Oklahoma, reflecting women's skills, their social standing, their aspirations, their pride and their bonds to each other. "Women did such things then," Hanners observed. "They needed these little bits of beauty."[19]

To compare, the traditional male Oklahoma memoir features larger-than-life men, while female Oklahomans most fondly remember the rare material comforts that made a lonely life bearable and the women who shared that loneliness with them. In doing so, they fashioned a literary genre of their own, one that speaks of grit and self-reliance, and of desperate men and the women who loved and resented them.

The wan and worried governor of Oklahoma has just informed cable television viewers that the situation in his state is dire. One quarter of a million acres have fallen to fire, evacuation plans are in full operation, and firefighters have been called in from neighboring states. No, not much ever changes in Oklahoma. Dust, drought, and fire still reign. No doubt, Oklahoma will continue to feed the dreams of many generations of writers to come. Meanwhile, *Children of the Dust* will satisfy those who hunger for genuine insights into the long, dark night of the Dust Bowl years.

LINCOLN, NEBRASKA, 2006

1. Donald Worster, *Dust Bowl: The Southern Plains in the 1930s*, 3–8.
2. Phyllis Cole Braunlich, *Haunted By Home: The Life and Letters of Lynn Riggs* (Norman: University of Oklahoma, 1988) 3–19, 49, 56, 61.
3. Ibid., 18, 48, 53.
4. Ibid., 49, 77, 80, 95.
5. Ibid., 21.
6. John Howard Payne and Grant Foreman, *Indian Justice: A Cherokee Murder Trial at Talequah in 1840* (Norman: University of Oklahoma Press, 2002); Douglas Gomery, "Will Rogers," in David J. Wishart, Ed., *Encyclopedia of the Great Plains*, (Lincoln: University of Nebraska Press, 2004) 278.
7. A. B. McDonald, *Hands Up! Stories of the Six-Gun Fighters of the Old Wild West* (New York: A.L. Burt Company, 1927) Forward, n.p..

8. Paul McClung, *Papa Jack: Cowman from the Wichitas* (Norman: University of Oklahoma Press, 1976) viii.

9. Robert K. DeArment, *Alias Frank Canton* (Norman: University of Oklahoma Press, 1996)151–52.

10. John Steinbeck, *The Grapes of Wrath and Other Writings, 1936–1941*(The Library of America, 1996) 211–692.

11. John Steinbeck, *The Harvest Gypsies: The Road to the Grapes of Wrath* (Berkely: HeyDay Books, 1936, 1986); Geta LeSeur, *Not All Okies Are White: The Lives of Black Cotton Pickers in Arizona* (Columbia: University of Missouri Press, 2000).

12. David Siceloff, *Boy Settler in the Cherokee Strip* (Caldwell, Idaho: Claxton Printers, 1964) 78.

13. Ibid., 249.

14. Tracy Daugherty, *Five Shades of Shadow* (Lincoln: University of Nebraska Press, 2003) 2–3.

15. Ibid., 4–5. It could be said that Daugherty portrays Timothy McVey as the 'anti-idyllic man.'

16. Ibid., 16.

17. Diane Glancy, *Flutie* (Rhode Island: Moyer Bell, 1998) 5–7.

18. LaVerne Hanners, *Girl on a Pony* (Norman: University of Oklahoma Press, 1994) 62–63.

19. Ibid., 38.

Grant Family Tree

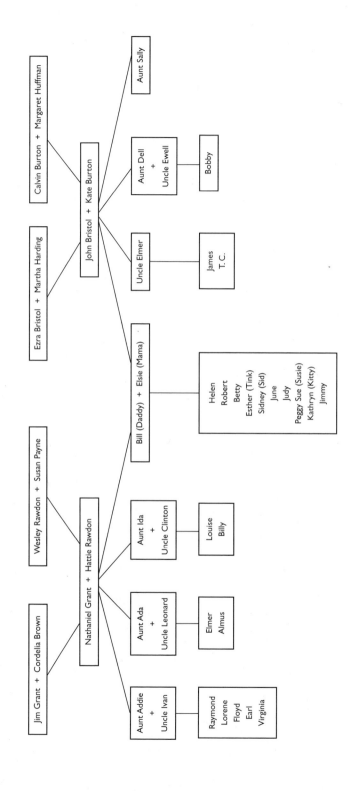

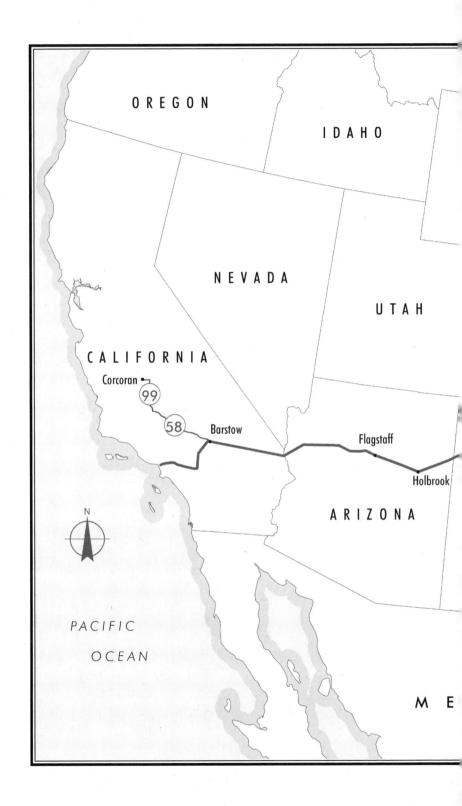

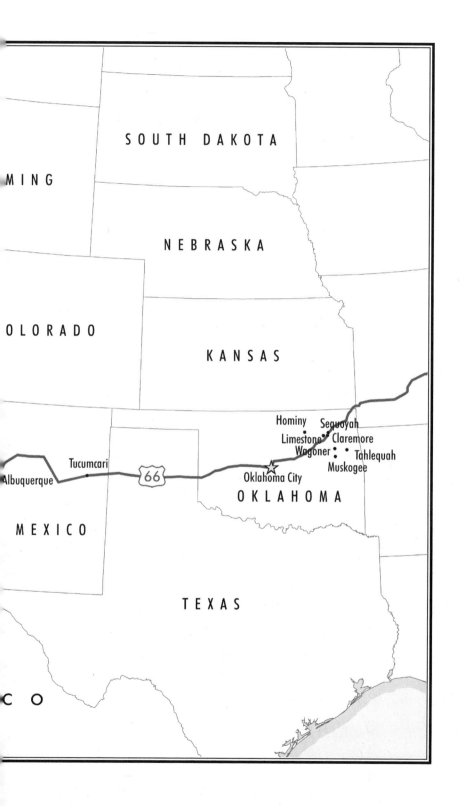

OKLAHOMA

Oklahoma

I DON'T REMEMBER when it began, but as far back as my mind can reach, Mama and Daddy talked about leaving the farm in Oklahoma and moving to California. Each season as the crops were gathered in, Mama's dreams were shattered as Daddy decided to stay and farm one more year.

I was still a toddler at the onset of a stretch of dry years that turned the Oklahoma prairie into a dust bowl, so I don't remember the first wave of migrants heading west, looking for a better life. That was when two of Daddy's sisters and their families left us for California.

Once Aunt Addie's family settled into their new life, she sent letters and postcards from California that created excitement in our house. Mama read them to us and showed us pictures of pink and white oleander bushes and bright bougainvillea vines trailing walls and fences. To me, the most exciting thing was a rock rising out of the ocean at Morrow Bay and a note on the back saying, "It took us forty-five minutes to climb to the top and back." Those letters fed Mama's imagination, and as I talked to her about California, Mama's dreams became my own.

The years of my childhood ticked away, and I watched cars and trucks traveling west on Route 66, sometimes as close as half a mile from our home. Then the war came, and more relatives sped away on passenger trains, and I longed to go west too.

I was almost fifteen when we finally left Oklahoma, and in the early morning darkness of that long-ago October day, I left behind a part of myself. Now when I look back, I'm thankful that Daddy waited, because he gave me a rare and wonderful childhood in the Oklahoma hills. There were lessons I would only understand after my journey on Route 66 and the backbreaking work in the sun-baked California cotton fields. Now I see how the important parts of who I am spring from the rich experience of those early years, when I was the child of farmers and a child of the land.

The Log Cabin

DADDY'S CHILDHOOD was marked by hardship. His mother, Hattie Elizabeth Rawdon, had owned a plot of land near Thayer, Missouri. Shortly after she married Nealie Grant, he sold the land to finance their first trip to the Oklahoma Territory.

In the years that followed, the couple traveled there and back in a covered wagon. Hattie became pregnant, gave birth, and buried all but five of eleven babies. It was on one of their return trips to Thayer, Missouri, in 1905 that my dad, Willie, was born.

Daddy recalled a scene at his grandmother's home as they left Missouri for the last time and headed for the newly established state of Oklahoma.

"I was five years old," he said, "and my daddy stopped the wagon in front of my Grandma Cotton's house. Mama begged him to go inside with her and say good-bye to her mother. But he just set there shakin' his head, with both eyes fixed on the road, and he never budged. Me and my sister Addie went inside with her and told our grandma good-bye. The two women cried. It was the last time they seen each other."

Their father's wandering caused desperate hardships on the family, and Daddy grew up determined that his kids would never know hunger or the loneliness of being without a home. Is it any wonder he was reluctant to pull his young family up and take off on a two-thousand-mile journey across five states, not knowing what lay ahead?

~

Unlike Daddy, Mama had a stable childhood. Grandpa Bristol was a farmer. She followed him on fishing trips, walking foot-logs over streams as my grandpa searched for a better spot to throw in their lines. On warm summer weekends, the family camped on the bank of the Verdigris River. Mama cut the legs off her brother's old overalls, dove into the water with her cousins, and learned to swim.

Camping came to an end when she married Daddy. He said, "Why sleep on the ground when you got a good bed at home?" Maybe he was thinking of the nights he slept on cold earth during his vagabond years.

Whatever the reason, when drought struck Oklahoma in the 1930's and thousands of farmers began the long migration to California, Daddy waited it out.

~

My earliest memories are of a one-room log cabin near Hominy, where we lived on Mama's Uncle Ari's place. A herd of cattle roamed the pasture in back of our house. A man came in a flatbed truck and threw blocks of hay to the cattle. He yodeled a lot.

One day the cattle got out and stampeded through our yard. My brother Robert pulled me into a chicken coop. I hunkered down with both feet on the ground. I peeked through the small door at the pounding hooves as they overturned boards and tin cans, tearing our playhouse to pieces. Mama came screaming from the cabin and pulled me and Robert to safety as the cattle spread in every direction.

~

Robert was born in that cabin in 1931. When I was born, in February 1933, we lived in an old house down the hill from Uncle Ari. Mama said I came into the world during one of Oklahoma's worst blizzards. Mama is part Cherokee, and Uncle Ari wanted to take her to the Indian hospital in Tulsa, but it was fifty miles away and they didn't have a good way to get there. It's too bad, really, because if she had gone, Uncle Ari would have registered her as a Cherokee, something she never did.

Mama said, "I watched big snowflakes float to the ground that afternoon as I went into labor. The two men drove into town for the doctor. The storm got worse. I thought Daddy would never get back. Mrs. Wells and Ida, Daddy's youngest sister, came home with him. Doc Jobin said he'd be out after he closed his office, but the snow drifted and he couldn't make it.

"That old house was so cold we couldn't heat it. Cardboard was nailed over cracks in the walls. The bed was in the corner across the room from the stove. You weighed ten pounds and I tore. There was nothin' to deaden the pain. It took a long time to heal because I didn't have stitches.

"Daddy worked hard helpin' deliver you, and the minute you cried, he cried too. It's something how fast a woman forgets the pain. When I saw you and Daddy, it was one of the happiest moments of my life.

"The two women wrapped you in a flannel blanket and left. Uncle Ari took them back into Hominy in the wagon. And the next day, Daddy and me cleaned you up with baby oil. You kicked and cried, but after we got you clean and warm, you snuggled up to me and went to sleep.

"The next winter, we moved back into the log cabin. It was smaller, but it was cozy and easy to heat."

❧

After we moved into the cabin again, my sister Tink was born. I had turned two years old a few months earlier. There's a story about that year that Mama liked to tell. Daddy was plowing not far from the cabin. At midmorning, Mama drew a fresh pail of water from the well. With a baby bundled in one arm and the bucket in the other, Mama kept an eye on Robert and me as we trailed along behind her down a dirt path.

Then, she said, "I missed the sound of your footsteps, and when I looked back, I froze! You were standin' over one of the biggest rattlesnakes I ever seen. He was coiled to strike and his tongue was goin' a mile a minute. His rattles sounded like a buzz saw. Robert and me had walked right past him, but there you stood, cool as a cucumber, lookin' him in the face. I thought sure that snake would strike.

"Daddy saw what was happening, and he said it almost scared him to death. He pulled the team to a halt and tossed the reins on the ground. Then he headed toward us. I laid Tink on the ground and tiptoed around behind you. Before Daddy got to us, I reached down and got a firm grip on the tail of your dress and throwed you over my head. I'll never know why that snake didn't strike.

"Daddy got a big rock and throwed it on him. He pinned the snake under the rock and killed it. It was as big around as my arm, with ten rattles and a button on the end of its tail."

I realize Daddy couldn't have allowed a rattlesnake to crawl around the field where he worked and Robert played, but that snake that could have taken my life didn't, and it always made me a little sad knowing it had to be killed.

⤳

The first three years of my life, Daddy sharecropped for Mama's Uncle Ari. Daddy said, "Ari didn't do much farmin'. Me and the kids done the work. Ari stayed drunk most of the time. He wasn't a bad person, he just couldn't stay away from whiskey. Aunt Al, she had a hard life with him."

Mama said, "Every time Aunt Al had a baby, Ari would go for the doctor. Then he would stay in town 'til it was all over and come home drunk.

"I helped her deliver her last baby. Ari left. When the baby was born, Aunt Al hemorrhaged and almost bled to death. She had a seizure. She groaned and throwed her head back. Ida, Daddy's youngest sister, was helpin' me. She flung both hands in the air and screamed 'Oh God!' and then took off and left me alone. I tore a rag from a sheet and rolled it up and stuck it in Al's mouth to keep her from swallowin' her tongue. I grabbed a wet rag and washed her face and held her 'til she stopped shakin'. It's a wonder she didn't die.

"After dark, Uncle Ari staggered into the house, drunk as usual. Al had seven babies, and he deserted her every time."

The Dust Bowl

IN THE MIDST of my parents' struggle to survive the Great Depression, drought struck the Oklahoma Panhandle. For five years it didn't rain enough to raise a decent crop. Great curtains of dust rolled across the prairie and surrounding plains states. A great migration of Okies began heading west. But not my parents— not yet.

Daddy said, "I watched the crops dry up and die. The corn stood there day after day with the sun beatin' down on it. Then the wind popped it loose from the ground and blowed the whole crop, I mean every stalk, right out of the field.

"It was a lucky day when I got a job with the W.P.A. I went to work on the roads and made a dollar a day. That year Ari didn't even buy seed."

"We didn't have no alarm clock," Mama said. "The roosters crowed and woke us up. One night a rooster crowed in the middle of the night. Daddy got up and walked out to the road and waited for his ride."

Daddy said, "I set down with my back against a tree. I pulled my coat around me and shivered until mornin'. The next Saturday, I went into town and bought a clock."

꒰

Daddy's sister Aunt Addie and her husband, Uncle Ivan, sold what they owned and traveled with their neighbors, the Foxes, helping with gas money. The two women and six kids rode in the back of an open truck for two thousand miles while the men took turns driving. After descending the steep grade that led off the Tehachapi Mountains and into the San Joaquin Valley, they bypassed Bakersfield and traveled north for another two hundred miles. Settling in the small town of Brentwood near San Francisco, they joined friends and family members who were already there, picking fruit.

Aunt Addie was too short to make money in the orchards. She couldn't manage the ladder or reach the fruit. She begged Uncle Ivan to move south to the Tulare Lake region where much of the nation's cotton crop was grown. She knew she could help if she could pick cotton. So they settled in the small farming town of Corcoran in the San Joaquin Valley, two miles from the levies of the Tulare Lake Basin. Then Aunt Addie began her long effort to lure Daddy to California.

A year later, Aunt Ada and Uncle Leonard moved to California. Mama said, "It just about killed Daddy to see Ada go. They were traveling with a friend in a 1928 Plymouth coupe. They stopped by the house to say good-bye and there were lots of tears. Ada rode in the rumble seat with her baby all the way to California. After she left, Daddy talked about leaving, but the time wasn't right.

"Ada and Leonard picked fruit for a while and then went to Corcoran, too. We felt left behind."

Pleasant Hill 1937

I WAS NEARING MY FOURTH BIRTHDAY when we moved from the log cabin to Duncan's Ranch near Wagoner. We moved into a rustic three-room house about half a mile from the main ranch headquarters. The big house, barns, and corrals were sprawled over several acres across the road from a one-room schoolhouse.

Daddy walked to work, too far away for us to play nearby. At day's end, Robert and I watched the road and raced to meet him. He joked with us as we followed him home, sometimes using a few words of Cherokee he had learned from Indian friends he hung out with in his single days. His favorite expression sounded to us like, "Challa cyskie." It made us laugh because we knew he was asking for a chew of tobacco.

One day we passed a shallow pond near the bottom of the hill. Daddy moved a rock in the edge of the water and upset two big crawdads that muddied the water, scampering for cover. At home he told Mama to take us down the next day to catch supper.

After breakfast the next morning, Robert and I hurried ahead of Mama and Tink, anxious to get our feet in the water. Mama waded in barefoot, lifted a rock, and uncovered half a dozen crawdads about five inches long, with long pinchers similar to a crab's. I tried to grab one but soon gave up. Robert reached for one but when it spread its pinchers and scooted away, he jumped and fell backward in the pond.

Mama picked them up from behind, throwing them in a bucket one by one while we waded. At home she coated the crawdad tails with a batter of flour, cornmeal, and milk and fried us a feast.

⌀

One day Mama, Robert, Tink, and I took a shortcut through the pasture, and a white-faced bull chased us. Mama always liked to tell this story. "That bull must've spied your red sweater, Betty. He pawed the ground and took off after us. I picked Tink up and grabbed Robert's hand, yelling, 'Hurry, Betty, get under the fence!' You ran fast, hit the ground, and rolled under the wire. I stood Tink over the fence and lifted the bottom wire for Robert. When I landed on the other side, that ornery bull was right on my heels. Robert screamed, 'Mama, my pant leg's caught.' I dragged him through the fence away from the bull and split his leg open on the barbwire. He was too heavy for me to carry. The four of us ran for the house, leavin' a trail of blood on the path."

At home Mama pried open a can of Raleigh Salve and rubbed it into the gash on Robert's leg before binding it with a clean white dishrag. Those big cans of salve, sold by the Raleigh man who traveled all over the country in those days, were used on cows, horses, chickens, dogs—and little boys. Every farmhouse had one on hand.

⌀

The weekend of July 25, Grandma and Grandpa Bristol came to visit in a Model A Ford filled with relatives. Uncle Elmer had brought my grandparents along with his family for the weekend. They brought armloads of fresh vegetables from their garden.

Late that afternoon, Mama went into labor. Daddy started down the road to get the midwife, with Grandma at his heels, arguing that Mama needed a doctor. Daddy got so mad he told her she ought to go back home. She wasn't going to leave and he knew it. They locked horns a lot but in some strange way, they respected each other. And I'm sure she was a lot of help through that long night.

The next morning Daddy led us into the bedroom and we climbed up on Mama's bed to see a baby boy in her arms. She named him Sidney Ray, after her friend's brother who had been killed in a knife fight over a girl at a local barn dance.

︾

Summer ended, and Robert started first grade. It was a half-mile walk to school and he was afraid to go alone, so Mama sent me with him. We followed a graveled road through the trees. At the top of the hill, behind a rock fence, stood a big white schoolhouse. Robert led me up a flight of stone steps into the school yard, and we entered a noisy room filled with kids we didn't know. A stranger sat behind a wooden desk at the front of the room. I watched a boy in baggy pants blow a spit wad and hit Robert in the face. I yelled at him and he said, "I didn't do nothing."

Another boy said, "Charlie, you're lyin'."

Then Charlie said, "If I 'as a lion, I'd eat you up," and he laughed, and that made Robert laugh, and the boy, and the man at the desk, and me, too, and I thought this might not be a bad place to be.

Robert handed the man Mama's note, which probably said something about like this: "Robert is the first one of our kids to start school and he's a little scared. Do you reckon it would be all right if his sister stayed and walked home with him, maybe just for a few days?"

The teacher, whose name was Mr. Gore, asked Robert how old he was, and Robert said he was six and that he didn't want to go to school. Mr. Gore said he thought things would work out. He found a double seat for Robert and me and gave me some crayon stubs and paper.

First through eighth grade students attended the one-room schoolhouse. One first grader was eighteen years old, a thin dark Indian woman named Rachel Rabbit, a full-blood Cherokee. She was Charlie's big sister, and she was learning to read and write.

I watched as Robert learned to write his name and I tried to copy his letters. One day Mr. Gore walked by and asked me what I was making. I said it was a three.

"And what's that?"

"A one."

"Do you like making numbers?"

I said I did.

He told Robert to stop by his desk at the end of the day for something to take to our mama.

At four o'clock, Charlie Rabbit, who was a sixth grader, rang the bell. He dashed up the stairs to the tower, grabbed the rope with both hands, and swung with all his weight. The big iron bell swung back and forth, BONG! BONG! signaling the end of another school day, and every kid dashed for the door.

I cried out, "Robert! Wait!"

Mr. Gore called him back too. He stuffed a note in my pocket and told Robert not to let me lose it because it was for our parents.

When Daddy got home that evening and read the note, he laughed. "What do you know?" he said. "Do you reckon she can keep up?"

Mr. Gore was going to let me be a first grader, just like Robert, and he had written my parents to say I needed a workbook.

Daddy said he had never got over having to quit school. He was in fifth grade when his daddy took him out to work, and he said, "He never knowed how much it hurt me. I liked learnin' and I liked being with other kids. If Betty can stay up with the first graders, we can manage a workbook." He told Mama, "Save the eggs this week. I'll go into town on Saturday."

Monday morning, I walked up the hill hugging my very own book and pencil. I was in first grade.

Each morning I knelt in front of Mama as she held me between her knees to comb the tangles out of my long hair. I cried and wiggled to get loose, but she held on and made me a beautiful French braid. She said I wore her out with my tender head and threatened to cut my hair, but Daddy said, "It's a sin for a woman to cut her hair. That's what the Bible says." Daddy's faith was important to him. He didn't go around preaching about it, we just knew. And Mama seldom went against anything he said. She went right on swatting me to sit still, and braiding my hair.

Then one morning after I left for school, Tink made a big scene as she got her hair combed, and it was just one time too many for Mama. She tossed the comb aside and picked up the scissors. When I got home from school, there was Tink with her short hair and her big black eyes. She looked like a doll and I wanted short hair too. But Mama said no.

When Daddy got home that evening, Mama cried and told him what happened. "I was ready to cut Betty's hair. She's the one who hates it so much. I couldn't see punishing her and myself anymore. But after I cut Tink's hair and seen all them pretty clumps of hair laying on the floor I thought, 'Oh God, what have I done?'"

Daddy said, "What's done is done, and Tink's hair will grow back." But they agreed not to cut my hair. It was past my waist before it was ever cut. When I was in eighth grade, Tink and I were finally able to wear our hair cut to our shoulders.

Muskogee 1938

WHEN I WAS ALMOST FIVE YEARS OLD we moved to Houseman's Dairy on the outskirts of Muskogee. Across the road and up the hill was Bacone Indian College with its impressive row of red brick buildings standing out. Our home was a small but comfortable two-room cottage not many yards from the main house. Mama put me on the school bus with Robert, but the teacher sent me home with a note saying I'd have to come back next year, when I was six. "City schools sure are different from the country," Mama said.

Tink and I spent a lot of time with Daddy in the milk barn at the dairy. It was the only time I ever saw him use a milking machine. He put feed in the cow stalls and sometimes cleaned them. The barn had a dirt floor that smelled of cottonseed meal and hay and manure. We sometimes followed him across the driveway and down a long row of cement steps leading to the basement under the house. Huge tubs were set up for washing and sterilizing utensils. Daddy and Mr. Houseman filled two ten-gallon cans with fresh milk and set them out for a big truck to pick up and haul into the creamery in Muskogee.

Robert and I especially liked twelve-year-old Sonny Houseman. Sometimes we went with him to dig sassafras. He carried a gunnysack and a small shovel and led us across a meadow behind the dairy barn where bushes grew along the railroad track. He dug the roots loose, and we pulled them out of the ground, broke the tangled pieces apart, and stuffed them into a sack. Sassafras tea was used for medicinal purposes. I thought it was horrible. It tasted like boiled tree bark.

One day I realized I hadn't seen Sonny in a while and I asked Mama where he was. She said his mother had taken him on the train to a place called the Mayo Clinic. When he came back, he stayed in his house, usually in bed. Mrs. Houseman asked Mama if I could come over to visit him. I sat beside him on his bed, sharing his coloring book. Sometimes we ate gumdrops shaped like orange slices. When he got tired, she would send me home and then send for me again the next day.

Then one night there was a loud knock at the door and I heard Mr. Houseman tell Daddy, "Bill, Sonny's gone." The men talked in a low tone and I could tell they were both crying. I heard Mama crying too. I hadn't understood that Sonny was sick enough to die.

⌇⌇

Since it was a good cash crop, Daddy was always looking for a place where he could raise a good patch of cotton. We stayed at the dairy less than a year, then moved about five miles out of Muskogee into an old two-bedroom house on the bank of the Verdigris River. Daddy said the land was rich and he thought if he helped Mr. McRevey raise a good crop for a year, he could buy a car, then start saving money so we could move to California, where the winters weren't so cold. He said, "I had to break ice so the cows could drink this mornin'. I'm tired of snow and ice."

Just beyond our backyard, trees lined the riverbank. The ground sloped about twenty feet to a six-foot drop-off bordered with small bushes. Below was a narrow sand bed and then the water's edge. Mama warned us away from the bank beyond the trees.

Robert, Tink, and I played with a red wagon near the house. One time Robert got in the wagon and Tink pushed him down the slope. She got it rolling but then it wouldn't stop. It raced across the slope, heading right for those bushes while both of them screamed. It hit the bushes and tumbled over the bank toward the river.

Mama heard the noise and came running out the back door. She scrambled through an opening in the trees, digging her feet into the sand and holding onto tree limbs as she climbed down the steep bank. Tink and I scooted along behind her. Robert was sprawled in the sand, and the wagon was on its side at the water's edge.

I thought Tink had killed our brother, but as Mama knelt over him, Robert opened his eyes and struggled to get up. He was scraped and bruised and covered with wet sand. He groaned as Mama helped him. Tink put her arms around his legs and squeezed. We made our way home, having learned our lesson about playing too close to the river.

∽

I turned six in February, and I talked Mama and Daddy into letting me go to school with Robert on the Monday following my birthday. Mama said they'd send me home. Daddy said, "Maybe she's learned enough to keep up and go into second grade in the fall."

The teacher, of course, said I'd have to wait.

Since I was already there, I spent the day at a desk, and I made friends with the six-year-old girl who sat in front of me. When the teacher handed out papers, she gave me one too. I did the same work the others did and joined in games at recess. That night, Robert told Mama the teacher said I'd have to wait, but I said that was in the morning, and later she had said I was doing OK and could come back. I wanted to go to school so bad, I deceived them all and kept going. I don't know what the teacher thought, but she didn't say anything more, and I went into second grade in the fall.

∽

Mama had Grandma Bristol's old Singer sewing machine. She made dresses for Tink and me from printed flour sacks. One day Mr. McRevey remarked to Daddy that Mama was a fine seamstress, and he said, "I don't reckon I ever thought about it." Mac went on and on. He said his wife sewed, but nothing like my mama. He said his wife said my mama was an artist. And his wife started giving Mama pieces of material she didn't need, and Mama made good use of them. But Daddy had noticed. Sometimes he would remark, "My! What a pretty little dress you got on!" My guess is, he thought all women could sew and it was no big deal.

◈

Late in the fall I woke up one morning in a hospital bed. I must have wondered where I was and why I was by myself, but the first thing I saw on the nightstand was a coloring book and a box of crayons, and any worries I had disappeared.

Then I heard people talking in the hall. It was my mama trying to come in and a woman in a white dress telling her she couldn't because I was too sick.

The last thing I remembered was Daddy carrying me into a tall brick building. I had seen flowers blooming beside the walk and I pointed to them. That made Mama grab Daddy's arm and say, "She noticed the flowers!" I remembered Mama crying.

All night I had been vomiting. Early that morning Mr. McRevey took me and Mama and Daddy into Muskogee. The doctor said I was dehydrated and had to be hospitalized. He asked Daddy if he could pay the hospital bill.

Daddy said, "I got a load of cotton on the wagon ready to be hauled into the gin."

"Is that all you have?"

"Yeah, I sharecrop for McRevey and I get half. That load's mine."

The doctor told his nurse to fill out the necessary papers for Crippled Children's Fund. That foundation paid the doctor and the hospital, and Daddy got to keep his cotton.

Mama told me later that Daddy held me while they put an IV in my arm. She said I struggled and cried to get off the bed. I don't remember. She pleaded to stay with me, but the doctor said there was nothing she could do and told her to go home. She said, "There was nothin' I could do but go home and pray. I went out and walked the yard and prayed until finally I felt a great load lift and I just knew you would be all right."

A week later, when I was out of the hospital, Daddy led me to the front of the church. Brother Smith stood me on the altar rail and proclaimed me "The Miracle Girl." I didn't know what that meant, but I soaked up the attention. Then I went back and crawled under the bench with Tink and Sid, lay down on a folded quilt, and went to sleep.

～

Fall was turning to winter and a cold north wind blew as Mama washed a tub of clothes on the rubboard and hung them on the top wire of an electric fence, the only clothesline she had. Mr. McRevey turned it on occasionally to keep the cows in. That morning he was in his yard watching Mama hang wet diapers. He walked down to his barn and a few seconds later a jolt of electricity knocked her back from the wire.

Mama told Daddy about it. She said, "I kept on hanging clothes by throwin' them across and lettin' go before they touched the wire. They froze stiff as a board but they dried."

Daddy said, "I told him we ain't stayin' another year and he's been spiteful ever since."

Of course Mama took up the subject of California right away. Addie had told her Ivan didn't have any trouble finding work, and Addie was picking cotton. Mama said she could do that too.

Daddy said, "I know, Mama, but we can't buy a car this year." I wonder how he kept from losing hope, but he didn't. He said, "Crossing the Rocky Mountains is not a picnic, and I don't see doin' it this year. One of these days, you'll see, we're gonna cross them mountains. But not this year."

～

As Christmas neared, Daddy told Mama that Mac had said that if we picked his pecans, we could keep half, sell them, and get presents. Mama wanted to get baby dolls for us girls. She said they were only fifty cents, undressed, and she could make doll clothes.

The next morning we went down the riverbank and found pecans scattered all over the ground. Mama and Robert shook the limbs while Tink, Sid, and I picked up pecans and put them in a gunny-sack.

I watched Mama working on her knees and I wondered if she was sick. I knelt down by her to help. Her voice quivered as she said, "Go help Sid pick up them pecans over by him. He's just a little feller, but he works so hard." Then she stood up, closed her eyes, and sucked in a deep breath of air. Turning her back, she took one corner of her apron and wiped tears from her eyes.

It wasn't usual for Mama to cry, but I always knew what she was crying about. This time, I couldn't figure it out. Especially with Christmas coming, a time of the year she loved. I could tell something was wrong, but I didn't ask. I was a teenager before I talked to her about that Christmas we picked up pecans and I watched her cry.

Tahlequah 1940

IN 1940 WE LEFT MUSKOGEE and moved to the Cherokee hills near Tahlequah. On June 3, Mama gave birth to twins. Years later, she would say, "I just didn't see how we could feed one more. If I had known it was twins, I don't know what I would have done." That explained the crying.

Judy had a mass of black hair and big brown eyes. The small amount of hair June had was blond. To go with her little bit of fuzz, she had blue eyes so big that Daddy said she would have to grow out around them. Before long I couldn't remember when the twins weren't around. Sid, three years old, felt differently. He suggested Mama and Daddy could give them away. He had been the baby for three years, and it must have been traumatic for him. But I remember Mama still carried him on her hip a lot.

❦

We lived within walking distance of Grandma and Grandpa Bristol's house, so I got to spend nights with them often. Grandpa didn't talk much and was on his way to being totally deaf. Grandma yelled at him, even though he learned to read lips and could understand almost anything if you talked right into his face. But she was still yelling at him when he died at eighty-eight.

Grandma's sister, Aunt Bert, lived with them. She was in her early forties but had the mind of a child. After breakfast, she filled her corncob pipe with tobacco and the two of us headed outside and walked hand in hand across the yard, as Grandma's chickens crowded around our feet. Bert liked to settle into an old, weather-beaten chair in the corner of the yard that was made of narrow wooden slats and leaned to one side. It was situated under a bushy peach tree. There she lit her pipe and waved her hand at the chickens, calling out, "Shooo!"

In the afternoon she rested in her rocker on the front porch. She would tap her pipe on the rail and dump the ashes into the dirt, then motion me onto her lap, lock her arms around me, and we'd both fall asleep. She was fiercely protective of that rocking chair and pipe. Our twelve-year-old cousins, Bobby and James, knew it, and they liked to get hold of the pipe and hide it from her. Grandma finally threatened to send Bobby home to Muskogee for the rest of the summer if he didn't behave. I thought the boys were awful mean. They caused Bert to get mad and say things like, "Dod dam' 'ou. Dit outta here and leabe us 'lone." She threw her shoes at them and they ran and laughed, standing just out of reach, mocking her gibberish. I hated them for that.

I didn't know why James lived with Grandma and Grandpa. He called them Mommie and Poppie, just like my mama did. In time, Mama told me that James's mother, Mable, had married my Uncle Elmer when she was fifteen, and then had James that same year. Five months later she was pregnant again and she couldn't face it. Mama said, "Abortion was illegal but she tried to have one anyway. Nobody knew who did it, and it was botched. She lost blood and then got gangrene. By the time the doctor came, it was too late. Mable called Mommie Bristol before she died and asked her to raise the baby. From then on it was understood that James belonged to Mommie. He never knew another mother."

Mama said, "I was eleven years old and I got real attached to him. When Elmer remarried, there was no mention of James leavin' with him. He's a good boy, only when Bobby comes around he gets into mischief. Never with the thought of hurtin' anybody."

~~~

When the twins were a month old, we celebrated the Fourth of July at Grandma's house. Uncle Elmer and his family, who all lived on the same farm, came up the hill. Mama's sister Aunt Dell came with her husband, Ewell, and their five little girls, from Muskogee.

Daddy took his straw hat from a nail beside the door and Mama tied her sun bonnet under her chin. Each of them carried a baby as Robert, Sid, Tink, and I raced down the gravel road in our bare feet until we reached our grandparents' house.

Bert rocked on the porch while the women prepared dinner and the men climbed the fence into the tobacco patch next to the yard. They gathered a few dry leaves, crushed them in the palms of their hands, and either filled a pipe or stuffed a chunk under their bottom lip. Daddy had given up tobacco when I was two years old, but he gave Bert a handful and joined the other men on the front steps. About that time James and Bobby sneaked around behind Bert's chair and slid a lighted firecracker underneath it. A few seconds later it went off.

Bert threw both her feet in the air, rocked backward until I thought she would turn over, and screamed and swore. The louder Bert cussed, the harder those boys laughed.

The screen door flew open and Grandma sailed across the porch with a broom in her hand. She chased the boys out of the yard. Uncle Elmer said, "Ah, come on, Mommie, the boys is just havin' fun."

"Fun my eye," Grandma said. "Bert could get hurt. Just yesterday, you was gonna take your belt to both of them for gettin' the dogs into a fight. You protect your dog better than you do Bert. I ain't puttin' up with this. You hear me? I ain't puttin' up with it no more. They either behave or I won't let them back in the yard and they'll do without dinner!"

Daddy stood at the top of the steps and kept watching both Grandma and Uncle Elmer. He didn't say a word, but as Grandma walked past him, he patted her shoulder and smiled.

❧

Later that summer we joined our grandparents and others for a big dinner on the banks of Dog Creek. Grandpa picked us up Sunday morning, except for Daddy, who was in the field. He didn't work on the Sabbath, but he didn't want to go to the picnic because he didn't like big gatherings. The whole extended family was there when we arrived. There was a big campfire going and Grandma was boiling corn and potatoes. Aunt Dell had brought apple pies and Mama had made blackberry cobbler. All the cousins spent the morning wading in the shallow spots in the stream.

As noon grew near, Mama sat on a quilt with the babies and kept an eye out for Daddy, hoping he would walk over for lunch with us. She kept looking in the direction of the field. Finally, he appeared through the trees and her face brightened. She took her shoes off and waded across the creek to meet him.

Aunt Bert brought a denim quilt made from old overalls and khaki pants, and she spread it on the ground and plopped down on it. She stuck an old pillow under her head and stretched out. Bobby and James came over quietly and picked up both sides of the quilt, causing Bert to roll to the middle. She screamed. Uncle Elmer joined the boys in swinging the quilt with Bert on it, taking her toward the swimming hole. They were laughing and counting as if they were getting ready to drop her into the water.

Bert screamed and begged, and Daddy motioned to Robert and our cousin T.C. They and Grandma grabbed the quilt. Daddy pulled Bobby loose and shoved him into the creek. James tried to get away, but he didn't have a chance. Grandma caught him and held him. "Here he is, Bill. Teach them a lesson." James hit the water with a splash. Uncle Elmer retreated. Bert laughed hysterically as the boys pulled themselves from the creek dripping wet.

When Grandma said, "The fun's over. Dinner's ready," Uncle Ewell and Aunt Dell settled on the ground beside our quilt. Uncle

Ewell asked Daddy how the crops were and Daddy said, "Not very good. A man can't raise a decent crop in these rocks."

Aunt Dell looked at Mama and said, "That little old house you live in must be awful crowded, Elsie."

"It ain't bad," Mama said.

"Don't the kids have to carry water from the landlord's well? How do you keep up with diapers?"

"I manage."

Then Uncle Ewell got to the point. "Them twins is pretty babies, Bill, but it must be an awful burden trying to raise two more with the four you already got. Why don't you let me and Dell take one home with us? We'd be glad to raise one of them just like it's our own."

Uncle Ewell was a plumber and owned a beautiful two-story house in Muskogee. All the upstairs bedrooms had balconies. I loved to lean on the carved, white rails and look out over the neighborhood at kids skating and playing hopscotch. It felt like the top of the world. They had Bobby and five daughters. But Aunt Dell was grieving over the loss of a baby girl who had died from pneumonia.

Mama looked at the babies sleeping snugly next to her. "Dell, do you honestly believe I could choose between my babies? Do you think I could part with either one of them?"

Daddy patted Mama's shoulder. "Don't worry. Ain't nobody gonna take our babies." Then he said, "We don't need no help raisin' our kids."

I was seven years old. I felt Daddy's anger. I knew he would protect us. I didn't think we were crowded. I was never hungry. Why would anyone want to take one of our baby sisters away from us?

Aunt Dell said, "Now, Bill, Ewell and me didn't mean no harm. We know all about that colored woman the county sent out to help Elsie. You'd rather take charity than let family help."

By now Mama was in tears. "Ruby Nave is a fine woman," she

said. "Betty and Tink's a big help, too." She wiped tears and smiled. "I got a good rockin' chair. I push it up to the wall and put one of the babies in Tink's arms and she kicks the wall with her feet. She ain't but five years old, but she can quiet a cryin' baby. These babies know her. After they're fed, they snuggle up to her and go to sleep. All four of our kids love these babies and they all like Ruby Nave too. They spend the whole day helpin' her." The subject was closed.

It had been a lucky day for us when Ruby Nave knocked on our door. June and Judy were less than a week old. Mama was still in bed. It was early June and school was out. I'd just helped with breakfast, making a pan of biscuits and scrambled eggs with salt pork drippings. Daddy left for the field and I was washing dishes, looking out the window, when I saw a tall black woman walking up the road. To my surprise she came right up to our door. I whispered to Mama, "It's a colored woman."

Mama said, "Well, tell her to come in."

I opened the door and the strange thin woman stepped inside. Her dark hair was pulled off her face and tied back in a bunchy ponytail. One eye was milky gray. She wore a faded housedress that reached below her knees, like one that Mama might wear.

She introduced herself and told us the county office had sent her on the doctor's recommendation because he thought we could use some help.

Mama said, "Oh, what a blessing! I need help so bad!" She motioned Ruby closer as she breastfed June. "I got my hands full, I sure do. They're good babies, and the older girls help, but there's only so much kids can do."

Ruby looked at the babies. "My, my, they don't look like twins, now do they? Yes, ma'am, you got this one and you got that one, now, don't you?"

Both women laughed and instantly they were friends. Ruby said, "Where would you like me to start?"

Mama thought for a few seconds and then she explained about the water situation. We didn't have a well. There was a big wooden barrel at the corner of the house for rainwater, but there hadn't been any rain. We had been carrying muddy wash water from the pond to fill the barrel, then carrying drinking water from the neighbor's well.

So we kids took off with Ruby to the pond with empty four-pound lard buckets. Ruby helped us fill them and put the lids on. We made a race of getting back to the barrel, and by the time we were finished, we all loved her. Mama got out of bed and scooped warm ashes from the stove. Ruby poured them into the murky water. As the ashes settled, they carried the mud to the bottom, and the water cleared.

Next Ruby built a fire under the iron kettle in the backyard and filled it with clean water. When the water was hot, she filled the washtub, warning us to stay back so we wouldn't get burned. She washed diapers on a rubboard. Tink and I rinsed them in a tub of cold water, wrung them out by hand, and hung them on the clothesline. I tried to use the rubboard like Ruby did and skinned my knuckles. It was the first of many times.

She helped us all that summer. We shelled and roasted corn and watched it crack and pop over hot coals. It was fun to eat. We helped get the work done, and Ruby made us part of it while letting us be kids at the same time. She was a rare person, one of those who truly touches your heart. I don't know how many times I heard Mama say, "What would I have done that summer without Ruby Nave?"

Aunt Sally graduated from high school, still living at home with Grandma and Grandpa Bristol. One Sunday morning I walked into her bedroom as she was putting on a pair of silk stockings. I said, "Why are you gettin' dressed up?"

She said John was coming to walk her to church. She gave me a shy smile and said, "John's special."

She sat down in front of her mirror and combed her short, blond hair. We heard John's voice, and on her way out of the room she said, "Here, I saved these for you." She handed me a wooden cigar box with an empty Blue Waltz perfume bottle and some broken beads I could string. The things my Aunt Sally saved for me were treasures, and I'm sure she meant for them to keep me busy while she greeted my soon-to-be Uncle John, but I put them down and quietly slipped across the room to get a glimpse of him. He opened the door, and they left for church ahead of the rest of the family.

Grandma put a clean dress on me and combed my hair. Uncle Elmer and his family joined us on our walk. We passed through a shady lane with tall trees on each side. Tree limbs lapped together above us and wild grapevines created a canopy over the lane. We came in sight of the church, and Mama and Daddy were waiting for us on the steps. Robert, Tink, and Sid ran to meet us, and we entered together.

The tiny white building with no steeple, cradled among the trees on a rocky hillside, was known as Paris Community Church. I asked Mama why it was called Paris. She said a prominent Cherokee Indian family named Paris had donated the land.

The congregation sang old songs like "Amazing Grace" and "When the Saints Go Marching In." But there was one song I heard at the Paris Church that I don't remember hearing anywhere else. Later I heard Mama sing it as she went about her daily chores. The words went like this:

> Talk it over with Jesus, and comfort will be found.
> Tell him all your troubles, whether day or night.
> Get your knees acquainted with the cold and rocky ground.
> Talk it over with Jesus. He will make it right.

Daddy complained about that rocky ground around Tahlequah. He said a man couldn't raise a decent crop there. As I listened to the

Paris congregation singing, I could almost feel the pain as I envisioned them kneeling among the rocks, their prayers curling like smoke, penetrating every tree and boulder in the rocky Cherokee hills.

⹌

Sunday dinner was at Grandma's house. Sometimes it was fried chicken. Sometimes it was beans and cornbread, fried potatoes and fried green tomatoes. She made her own pickles and sauerkraut in big wooden barrels, and we'd pick some out with a long iron fork that hung from a nail in the kitchen. She had sorghum molasses, too, stored in stone crocks. The sugarcane it was made from grew tall as corn, with a bushy head swaying above the stalk. Grandma and Grandpa used long sharp knives to cut the stalks and wouldn't let me get close, so I played along the edge of the field. They cut the stalks close to the ground and stripped away the long narrow leaves. Then they threw the stalks into a wagon and hauled them into the mill.

I liked to walk with Grandma to the sorghum mill and sample the juicy strips of sugarcane, and watch as they cooked down into a thick brown syrup. I thought Grandpa owned the sorghum mill, but Mama told me it belonged to a farmer who Grandpa called "Nigger Charlie." Whenever Grandpa took his cane in, Charlie sent his help home because Grandpa said he didn't want "no nigger's hands" in his molasses. On the other hand, Charlie, who sure was black, made the clearest and best molasses in the county. Grandpa wouldn't take his sugarcane to anyone else, and he had to compromise his prejudice for taste. So he worked with Charlie—but he made Charlie send the other workers home.

Grandpa fed the strips of cane into a press. It squeezed the sweet juice into a big metal pan with a fire underneath it. The pan had several sections. The juice cooked in the first one for a period of time and then was passed into the next and the next, and so on down the line until it boiled to the right thickness. Mama said, "When Charlie finished cooking it down, it was a pretty, clear amber color."

༃

When I spent the night with Grandma, I often ate her pancakes with molasses. One morning as I was finishing such a breakfast, I heard her scream. I ran out the door and through the front gate, catching up to her as we crossed the barnyard. She was yelling and waving her arms. "Get! Get away! Leave the baby alone!"

A little farther down the hill in the pasture, two big work horses were tromping a brown and white bundle on the ground. They reared up and came back down with their front feet, striking with bone-crushing force as Grandma cried, "Oh, dear God!" She picked up a big stick and motioned me back, then struck at the horses. She beat them away and I crept closer. Grandma leaned over the tiny body of a newborn calf. She sobbed and said, "It's the second one they killed this month. What are we gonna do with them mean horses?"

It worried her that I had seen such a thing at seven years old. She told me Grandpa would know what to do. She said maybe they could go in Uncle Elmer's pasture.

༃

Late that summer Daddy said, "We can't stay here no longer. I'm tired of plowing up rocks." He had been working for other farmers when he could, for a dollar a day. Then Uncle Clinton made a deal with Daddy to move onto his farm near Wagoner and help him. Uncle Clinton had raised a good crop, but Clinton's father, who owned the farm, was getting on in years and wasn't well enough to help.

Mama, of course, saw this as a good time to bring up California. She wanted to borrow money and go. She was sure Daddy would get a good job out there and pay it back right away. But Daddy didn't want to leave with a debt over his head, and he wanted a car. So after a little less than a year in the Cherokee hills, we moved again.

Wagoner

WHEN WE ARRIVED IN WAGONER we moved into another log cabin, with two rooms and a breezeway between. Aunt Ida's house was a short walk across a meadow and through the trees. It turned out we wouldn't live on Uncle Clinton's farm too long, and the time we were there we had more than our share of accidents and sickness.

Judy was on a bottle at night, the first time Mama had put a baby on a bottle. My parents thought goat's milk was closer to mother's milk than cow's milk, so Daddy bought a goat and milked her in the evening. We called the goat Nanny. She romped and ate everything in sight. She made a game of circling the rooms one by one and then shooting through the breezeway, baaing loudly. Nanny made a perfect figure eight and kept us laughing.

Daddy said there was lots of work in Uncle Clinton's fields, with harvest just around the corner. One field had a bumper crop of watermelons. Uncle Clinton bragged about his melons, and took a pickup load into town to sell. Our cousin Louise asked him, "Daddy, when are you gonna bring us a watermelon?" He said if he came across a busted one he'd bring it to the house.

Aunt Ida said, "Why wait? We'd all like some watermelon." But he couldn't stop bragging about his lucrative crop. Then one day nine-year-old Robert got us kids together and we went down to see what this big deal was all about. We gasped when we saw the plump green melons all over the field. We'd seen a few melons in Grandpa

Bristol's fields, but nothing like this. And I'd never seen a striped one.

Robert said, "Them striped ones are yellow inside." I had never seen a yellow watermelon. I carried one over to the edge of the field and dropped it on the ground. Then I dug into the heart, and with juice running down my arm, I ate the sweet yellow meat. We pulled ripe melons from the vines, carried them near the creek, ate the hearts out, and threw the rest over the bank. We helped ourselves until we couldn't eat anymore.

The next day Uncle Clinton found the watermelon rinds and the waste we'd left behind. He was over six feet tall, and he had the biggest feet I had ever seen. Sometimes he was as funny as a clown. But that day, when he stomped through our door, his big feet shook the house. He pulled his belt off. Louise screamed and ran. Aunt Ida rushed in from the kitchen and said, "What's going on?"

He bellowed, "They know what's going on! They sneaked into my watermelons, and I aim to teach them all a lesson!"

I was on the floor, frozen. Robert, Tink, and Sid were safe at home.

Aunt Ida told Uncle Clinton to put his belt away. She said, "You should have divided with the kids and then they wouldn't have had to steal from you. Besides, you better not lay a hand on one a Bill's kids. You go on now. You tell Bill and let him handle it. You ain't gonna use that belt on anyone in this house either. Bring a melon home once in a while!" At that, Uncle Clinton left, slamming the door so hard it seemed to shake the whole house.

When Daddy and Mama heard about what had happened, they laughed. Daddy said stealing was wrong and he didn't want it to happen again, but I heard him tell Mama that the season was going to be over and a lot of those fine melons were going to go to waste.

In September, Robert and I returned to Pleasant Hill School. Tink and Louise started first grade. Aunt Ida walked with us, and three-year-old Sid, along with Louise's brother, Billie, visited the school for the first time. We walked a half mile through the woods, following a well-trod path. Then we entered a clearing and there was the school, its tall bell tower still dominating the landscape.

We only stayed until noon that first day, but Sid tried every piece of equipment on the playground. He was bucked off the teeter-totter and knocked down by the merry-go-round. He fell into the dirt at the bottom of the slide. And then he did it all over again. Aunt Ida said he never cried, but he was one tired little boy by the time we were ready to walk home. He rubbed his eyes and whined and lagged behind. Finally Robert gave him a piggyback ride.

We were in sight of the cabin, with a fence to crawl under, when Sid slid to the ground. Aunt Ida lifted the bottom wire and he dropped to his hands and knees. He screamed with pain as the bone above his right wrist snapped. Aunt Ida cried out, picked him up, and ran for the house.

Mama was watching for us. She rushed through the tall weeds to meet us. Sid was holding his right wrist against his body and supporting it with his left hand. Mama took him in her arms. Aunt Ida said, "He played so hard today, do you reckon he hurt it on the playground and finished breakin' it when he tried to crawl under the fence just now?" Mama assured her it wasn't anybody's fault. Robert went for help. Daddy and Uncle Clinton took Sid to the doctor in Wagoner. When they came back, a big plaster cast covered his arm from his elbow down. While the rest of us were in school, Sid followed Daddy everywhere. Daddy said, "That broken arm ain't slowed him down a bit."

෩

Sid's office visit was the first in a stream of doctor's calls Daddy made that year. One day he came home with a fever after gathering corn all day. He said, "I ache all over. I'm afraid I got bit by a black widow."

Mama said, "Daddy, black widows are poisonous. Why didn't you come home?"

"Because Clinton needed me," Daddy said. "We need to get the corn in before the weather gets bad." Finally he couldn't do anything but groan. Again Uncle Clinton came to the rescue. He took Daddy to the doctor, who gave him an antivenom shot and pain medicine.

A couple of weeks later, Daddy found a tree the wind had blown to the ground. He hitched the horses to the tree and dragged it home for firewood. As he entered the yard, he got his foot tangled in the reins. The horses spooked and pulled him to the ground, dragging the log over his leg. The top of his leg was bruised and torn but he wouldn't go to the doctor. His leg got infected, so when he did go for help, the leg had to be lanced. He wasn't over that when mumps swept through the school and we brought them home. Everyone in the cabin had the mumps except Mama, who had had them when she was a little kid. Daddy's temperature soared and the glands in his neck swelled. Then he returned to the field too soon and had a relapse. The swelling went into his groin. He and Judy both had a rough time recovering. Judy still has a scar where the doctor lanced her neck.

༄

It's no wonder Mama worried so much. Times were hard and she worried that Daddy would die. She feared the loss of a child. Little by little it became a chronic thing, and I picked up on her fears. I began to think of how I would keep us together. I thought I would hide all of us kids in the woods, maybe in a cave where no one would find us, so that we wouldn't be separated. This was the beginning of chronic nightmares that plagued me throughout childhood.

The sickness passed that year and things returned to normal. Daddy helped Uncle Clinton finish bringing in the crops and then he was able to help another farmer, Henry Gore, gather in his cotton.

One Saturday morning I skipped around the hill just ahead of the other kids, headed for a little shack I spotted on the hillside. Daddy stopped me, calling, "Not so fast, Betty." I backtracked and followed him into the field.

I was nearing my eighth birthday and it was my first time to pick cotton. The field had been picked once, and most of what was left were cracked-open bolls. I pulled the hard, half-open bolls off and stuffed them into a gunnysack Mama had rigged up.

There was a small group of workers in the field, including a black woman with her two teenage daughters. The only black person I'd ever known was Ruby Nave. Those were the days when schools and neighborhoods were segregated.

Henry's three sons were helping, too, and it was midmorning before he parked his pickup at the field's edge. His son Will lifted the strap from his sack, dropped it on the ground, and walked across the rows of cotton toward the truck. Henry yelled, "What do you think you're doin'? Get back to work. We gotta get these bolls out of here today."

"Did you bring water? I need a drink," Will said.

"Get yourself a drink, and get that sack back on."

Henry passed over a couple rows and greeted Daddy. He said, "Glad you and your family could make it. I need the help."

Daddy said, "We can use the work. And I hear there's a rain comin' in. That means winter's already on us, don't it?"

Then I heard Henry say he'd been talking to his dad about us. "He's got a farm six miles out of Claremore and he needs a share-cropper. What do you think, Bill?"

"I've been looking for a place. I was hopin' we could get outta that cabin before winter."

"You'll like what he has to offer you. He bought some land from my wife's folks. They built her and her first man a two-story house, a good home, but when he died, she moved out. Said she couldn't live there no more. She won't live in it with me either. So Dad, he lets the sharecroppers live in that house. I'm goin' over tomorrow. Why don't you come and take a look?"

Daddy agreed, and I couldn't wait to get home and tell Mama.

I tried to picture the big house. I shut out everything around me. My mind was way out in the land of dreams when a piercing scream brought me back to reality. "Mama! Fire! Fire! Our house is on fire!" I looked up. The black woman and her two daughters dropped their cotton sacks on the ground and ran screaming and crying as flames leaped through the roof of the shack on the hill. Daddy, Henry, and the rest of the small crew hurried up the hill toward the fire.

When we reached the house, Daddy put his hand up and motioned Tink and me back. The day was cold but the fire's heat burned my face. I held my arm up in front of me.

Daddy grabbed the well rope, loosened it, and lowered the bucket, then he pulled it out filled with water. The men and boys formed a human chain, throwing buckets and cans of water on the fire, but it was no use. Flames leaped at them like they were magnets, and the intense heat drove them back. The boards of the old house were like paper, and, in a matter of minutes, the place had burned to the ground.

The widow and her daughters clung to each other and cried. "Dear God, what are we gonna do now? We ain't got nothin' but the clothes on our backs."

One of the girls said, "We got each other, Mama."

The older girl looked at her sister and said, "What will we do? Just you tell me? What do you think we gonna do?"

Daddy stared at the smoldering fire. Tears rolled down his face as he asked them, "You got any relatives close by?"

The woman said, "I got a brother just over the hill. We'll go there for now."

Everyone was standing around in shock and for a while no one spoke. Then Henry asked, "How far is it to your brother's?"

"It ain't far, Mr. Gore. We can walk it. But I reckon we'll just hang around here for a while. Seems like it's still home." And she moved closer to the smoldering heap. She was sobbing. "Don't seem right. This mornin' we had a home and now it's a heap a ashes."

Henry paid them for the work they had done that morning. He asked them again about the walk ahead of them, but the woman said the walk would do them good, and they went on their way.

ॐ

In the late afternoon we finished the field. Henry's truck was loaded with shriveled bolls that had cracked open and exposed the little cotton that was left. The last of the crop was ready to be ginned. Henry thanked Daddy and they shook hands. "You and my dad will get along fine," he said. "You'll find him to be a fair man. I believe the two of you can work out a deal that'll be good for both of you."

Robert, Tink, and I gave Daddy our little gunnysacks. He stuffed them inside his big canvas one, rolled it up, and put it under his arm. We stopped for a minute by the burned-out shack. Smoke drifted up from a couple of hot spots in the smoldering ashes. Daddy walked over and kicked at them. Then he said, "Let's go home," and with hurried steps he led us back to the road.

I caught sight of our cabin through the trees and ran ahead, flung open the door, and cried, "Mama, we're gonna move!"

"What do you mean!"

"Henry Gore's dad has a big two-story house, and he needs a sharecropper. Daddy's going with Henry tomorrow to talk to him."

Mama turned to Daddy and he told her what he had heard. He said she should go with him. We could stay with Aunt Ida. Mama was so excited, she said, "It would be so good if we could move into a big house."

I lay awake a long time daydreaming about it. I pictured a long front porch with tall pillars. I walked through the front door into a big living room, maybe with real wood floors that could be damp mopped to pick up dust. I could see a long winding staircase leading up to four bedrooms, with balconies off each one. There had to be balconies.

ॐ

The next morning, Daddy walked us to Aunt Ida's. He told us to be good and thanked her, saying he was sorry to trouble her.

She said, "It ain't no trouble, Bill. I want to see you and Elsie have a better place to live. I feel excited myself."

I stood in the window and watched him disappear through the trees. My hope was so high, the time dragged. I thought the day would never end. When at last they returned and Daddy came for us, I ran all the way home. As soon as I entered the cabin, I could see that Mama had been crying.

"Mama, what's the matter? Did you see the big house? Did Daddy talk to Grandpa Gore?"

"Yes, honey, but the people who live there ain't got no place else to go."

Daddy came in and I asked, "Ain't we gonna move, Daddy?"

He said, "We can't just force people out into the road. It ain't right."

The Montgomery family had five kids and Mr. Montgomery told Daddy he didn't know what they'd do if they had to get out. Mama said, "But, Daddy, it's a long while before plantin' time in the spring. They can find another place."

"Ain't there a pie supper Friday night?" Daddy said. "I'm plannin' on takin' Betty and Tink. Let's decide what kind of pies you're gonna make and worry about movin' after Christmas."

Tink and I looked at each other and smiled. This would be our first pie supper.

ॐ

A couple of days later, Daddy came home from town with groceries and two empty candy boxes. One read Baby Ruth, and the other read Butterfinger. Mama covered them with crepe paper. Tink's pie box was decorated in pink and mine in blue. Mama cut rose petals from crepe paper and curled the tip of each one with the scissors. Pressing the middle of each petal with her thumbs, she arranged them into a rose, tied the bottoms together with machine thread, and glued them on top of the boxes with paste made from flour and water.

Daddy and Aunt Ida searched through the apples on the storage shed floor. Some were bad and had to be thrown over the fence to the pigs. Others had bad spots but could be trimmed and salvaged. When we got home from school on Friday, the whole kitchen smelled of fresh apple pies, two for the pie supper and two for our family.

Years later I asked Mama how she could afford to decorate the boxes so nice and pretty. She said you could buy a sheet of crepe paper for a penny in those days. But Mama was an artist; she could always make something out of nothing.

∻

That night we left for the pie supper with our colorful boxes concealed with newspaper. No one was supposed to know which pie belonged to whom. Aunt Ida and Louise joined us on our walk through the woods.

When we reached the schoolhouse, a noisy crowd was already gathered inside. At the front of the room, pretty boxes decorated the floor at the edge of the stage. Uncle Clinton met us at the door and carried our pies to the front where he removed the paper and put them with the others. A few minutes later, he stepped up on the stage and said, "OK, folks, it's time to start the biddin'. Remember, every dime made here tonight will go to buy Christmas candy for the school kids." He held up a white box with yellow flowers and greenery and said, "Smells like chocolate to me. Or is it banana cream? Who'll give me fifty cents?"

And with that, the pie supper was under way. Most pies sold for a dollar or two. Uncle Clinton lifted Tink's pie above his head and said, "Look at them pretty pink flowers. I believe I can smell roses. Yep, sure enough, they're pink and white roses. Smells like apple pie, too." The bidding began and went higher and higher. I looked at Daddy, who was sitting near the back of the room. He humped his shoulders and winked at me, smiling. Tink's pie sold for five dollars.

When the bidding was over, the pies were cut and each was shared by the girl who brought the pie and the person who bought it. But no one went home hungry. All the pie boxes were empty except for a few crumbs.

Aunt Ida carried a flashlight as we walked back through the woods. An owl in the distance called, "Whoo! Whoo!" Tink cried and clung to Daddy, so he carried her home. We went to bed tired, already excited about Christmas, especially the school program.

❧

Daddy was cutting wood. Aunt Ida came walking toward our house at her usual fast pace. Daddy sank the ax into a chunk of wood, splitting it in half. He looked up and laughed. "What's the hurry?"

It was Sunday, December 7, 1941. The Japanese had bombed Pearl Harbor. "It's all you can hear on the radio," Aunt Ida said.

Daddy said, "What are you sayin'? We're at war? Where's Pearl Harbor?"

Mama was at the cabin door by then, listening, too.

Aunt Ida said, "It's in Hawaii, several hundred miles off the coast of California. They bombed our ships, and a bunch of our boys have been killed. They're talkin' about draftin' able-bodied young men."

Mama looked worried. "Did they say what age, Ida?"

"Now, Elsie, don't go gettin' yourself all upset," Daddy said. "They ain't gonna take a man away from his wife and six kids. You need to be worrying about what you're gonna do with all them rooms in that big house at Claremore."

"Are we gonna move, Daddy?" I was so excited about the big house, I forgot the war.

"I'm sure hopin' we get that house!" Mama said. For the time being, Daddy was able to convince her he would not be drafted. He buried the ax in a log and walked home with Aunt Ida to hear the news on the radio.

At school we practiced our Christmas program. Miss Duval, our teacher, helped us organize a rhythm band. We were twelve in all, each with a simple percussion instrument. Robert beat the tambourine, Tink kept time with rhythm sticks, and Louise played sleigh bells. The school gave us uniforms. Miss Duval chose me to lead the band, so I had a tall hat. The night of the program, I stepped to the front of the stage, announced what we were about to play, and bowed. As my hat tipped and fell down over my face, I heard a loud roar in the back of the room. I'd recognize that laugh anywhere; no one else sounded like my Uncle Clinton.

Near the close of the program, Santa Claus came down the stairs with a sack on his back overflowing with bags of candy, apples, and oranges. Aunt Ida pulled at his beard and said, "Hey, Santie Claus, I been a good girl."

Santa laughed and I said, "That ain't Santa Claus. That's Uncle Clinton."

Louise said, "That's not my daddy. You're just mad 'cause you don't believe in Santa."

"There ain't no real Santa Claus."

"Is too!" she cried, and ran to her mama.

Uncle Clinton stayed to help clean up and took the Santa suit home with him. Christmas Day, Louise rushed to our house to tell how she had been awakened on Christmas Eve by someone prowling around in the living room. She sneaked out of bed and watched Santa fill her stocking and leave gifts on the floor near the big potbelly stove. Daddy said, in a low tone, "Let her believe in Santa Claus if she wants to."

Then, after Louise left, he said, "I'll tell you what Santa Claus is. One Christmas Eve, I was about six years old, my mother put us to bed and told us we weren't gonna get anything for Christmas because there wasn't any money. After we went to sleep, Aunt Norrie walked over to our house. She bought us each an apple, and everything she needed to make a big batch of chocolate candy. The next mornin' when we woke and found all them goodies, we was sure Santa Claus had remembered us. And after that, no one could convince me Santa wasn't real. I know what Santa Claus is."

It was the day after Christmas when a box arrived in the mail from Aunt Addie in California. She sent two dozen baby diapers, paper dolls, and coloring books. The box was filled with goodies. She wrote a long letter still pleading with Daddy to move to California. She sent a picture postcard showing fields of fluffy white cotton, and she promised there was work.

Mama said, "Did you ever see such a pretty field of cotton? I bet I could pick two hundred pounds a day there."

Daddy said, "I never seen cotton like that before. I hear they grow fine cotton crops in the South, but I didn't know they raised it in California. If we move to Grandpa Gore's place, maybe we can save enough money so we can move there next year."

In early January, the weather was cold and we were low on firewood. Daddy hitched up the horses and helped Robert and me on their backs, and we rode toward the spring where we got our water. We found a tree on the ground. Daddy trimmed the tree with the ax and rigged it up so the horses could pull it home.

We neared the cabin just as a pickup turned off the main road and drove down the hill. Henry Gore stopped the truck and leaned out the window. "Ready to move, Bill?"

"Yeah. That cabin gets colder every day. Have them folks found a place?"

"They're movin' into an old house down the hill from the big one. My dad told them they could stay there 'til they find somethin' else. You folks can move in this weekend."

Mama was listening from the door of the cabin. "You hear that, Mama?" Daddy said.

She smiled and said, "I heard!"

I jumped up and down and yelled, "Yeah! I knowed we was gonna move."

Henry laughed. "I'll be here with my truck early Saturday mornin'." With that, he started his pickup. His son Will waved to us as he drove away.

Sequoyah

IT WAS ABOUT SIX O'CLOCK in the morning, and the fire Mama built in the kitchen stove had already warmed the cabin. I could hear the chickens squawking as Daddy and Robert rounded them up and tied their legs together for the long ride to Claremore. Mama said, "It's time to get up, girls." June and Judy squirmed and rubbed their eyes as we gathered around the table to eat a hot breakfast of scrambled eggs, biscuits, and gravy. Mama kept nudging us to hurry. When Henry and Uncle Clinton arrived around eight, she shuffled us six kids out the cabin door and helped us into the two pickup cabs while the men loaded our few belongings.

Robert, Sid, Tink, and I crowded in with Uncle Clinton for the forty-mile trip that seemed like an eternity. When at last the two trucks bounced through Claremore, we turned north on Route 66 and followed the famous highway for six miles. Sequoyah's two-story brick schoolhouse came into view as it stood out against the cold winter sky. Robert said, "What's that long wooden building beside the school?"

Uncle Clinton said it was a gymnasium where they played basketball, and maybe the high school was in it, too. This made Robert hang his head and say, "That's where we're gonna go to school." Moving and changing schools were hard for him. Just when we would get settled in one place, we'd move again. Tink and I had each other, but Robert was alone, and he stayed to himself a lot.

Henry led us down a gravel road past a couple of small farms.

U. S. DEPARTMENT OF LABOR
UNITED STATES EMPLOYMENT SERVICE
APPLICANT'S IDENTIFICATION CARD

Case Number R-345   Identification Number 4257-1163

Name Bill Grant

Address Gen. Del., Hominy

Age 29   Height 5'6"   Weight 128

OCCUPATIONAL CLASSIFICATION
Laborer

Registration Date	Referrals to Projects	Foreman or Supervisor
12-5-33 Renewal Dates		
	Project	Assigned
	Interviewer	Released
	P.	A.
	I.	R.
	P.	A.
	I.	R.
	P.	A.
	I.	R.

NOTICE TO EMPLOYERS: The Applicant named hereon has not been referred by this office unless he presents also a card of introduction. This is only an identification for work on WPA and PWA projects.

Bill Grant's United States Employment Service Applicant's (WPA) Identification Card, 1933.

Robert, upper left; Louise, lower left; Tink, bottom, third from right; and Betty, standing in front in tall hat; 1941.

Daddy and sisters, Ada and Ida, 1943.

Robert and Mama, 1942.

Daddy and Grandpa Bristol (right), 1942.

Daddy and Mama, 1946.

Daddy, Mama, and Kitty, 1946.

Tink, Betty, Mama holding Kitty, Judy, Sid, and June (bottom row), 1946.

Robert and siblings, 1946.

Sid on Daddy's horse, 1946.

Uncle Ed and Aunt Jane, 1947.

The winter fields were bleak and bare. Tall weeds along the fences had died and fallen to the ground. Next we turned onto a dirt road and drove down a long lane. Sensing we were getting close, I kept my eyes on the road ahead. Both pickups entered a long driveway, and there it was—a tall, yellow house, half-hidden in the trees. There was white trim around the upstairs windows, but no balconies. That didn't dampen my excitement, though.

Uncle Clinton parked beside a picket fence. There were thorny rose branches growing between the white boards. Daddy unlatched a wooden gate and we entered the yard. A path led to a long front porch with tall pillars.

The door opened and a short, stocky man smiled and greeted us. "Come on in, folks." It was Grandpa Gore, Henry's father.

I looked around the big empty room with its tall ceiling and dark wooden floors. "My goodness, Mama, what are we gonna do with all this room?" Daddy said.

We could hear voices coming from a room beyond the kitchen. "We must be early," Daddy said. "Sounds like the Montgomerys is still here."

Grandpa Gore said, "We're doin' some work on the other house. They've moved some stuff, but they ain't left yet. Hope you folks don't mind if they stay in that room for a couple of days."

"If we'd knowed, we'd have waited 'til next week," Daddy said. But we were there and the only thing to do was unload and set up our beds.

I asked, "Where's the stairs?" Mama led us into the next room. There, beside the cookstove, was a steep cased-in stairway leading up from the kitchen. Robert, Tink, and I raced up the steps with Sid at our heels. We reached a landing and hurried toward the three empty rooms. Ah! There was my balcony. A wooden banister the length of the hallway protected us from falling over the edge. Mama's voice came up behind us. "Robert, Betty, listen to me!" We rushed to the top of the stairs. She said, "Don't you ever run up them stairs like that again. Do you hear me?"

I leaned over the rail. "Why?"

Daddy stepped to the foot of the stairs. "Don't question your Mama. Just do what she says. Don't play on the stairs. Take a good look. If you fell from up there, you'd tumble all the way to the bottom. Now, come back down here and behave yourselves. Robert, I need you to help me unload the stuff."

The Montgomerys stayed three days. On the third day I followed Robert as he helped them move into the house at the bottom of the hill. Beside the weather-beaten house was a dump filled with old bottles, tin cans, and rain-soaked papers. The grayish brown wood on the outside of the place looked cold and dreary. A sad feeling swept over me as I realized why Daddy was concerned about that family. I was anxious to go back up the hill.

We settled into the big house with so much excitement I almost forgot about California for a while, but Mama kept us reminded as she spoke of spring and the idea of raising a good crop so that we could move west.

The Montgomery kids walked to school with us for the next few weeks. War was always in the news, and they were drafting young men all around us. It was also a constant topic at school and home. Classes began each morning with the Lord's Prayer and flag salute. One day at an assembly in the auditorium, I noticed the oldest of the Montgomery kids, Joe Bob, stood with his head down as students all around him saluted the flag. His sister, Betsy Ann, was in my class, but I had never noticed that she didn't join the rest of us in the Pledge of Allegiance.

Daddy came in from the field one evening soon after and said, "Mama, Mr. Gore told me the Montgomerys don't believe in salutin' the flag. Now the kids can't go to school no more if they don't do the flag salute with the other kids."

"Must be their religion," Mama said. "Don't seem right, punishin' little kids because of their mama and daddy's religion."

"Grandpa Gore says it's the law."

The next morning, we all sat quietly while the teacher helped Betsy Ann clean out her desk. A few minutes later, Mr. Montgomery and his son came to the door of the classroom. Joe Bob had his arms full of books. Everyone watched as Betsy picked up her school work and hurried toward the door. He was twelve and she was nine. A few weeks later, the family moved. I often wondered if those kids ever went back to school. They weren't the only children in the country to be expelled for their silence during flag salute. They probably were Jehovah's Witnesses. That church did not allow children to recognize the flag, and many children were removed from schools. Lawsuits went all the way to the Supreme Court, and in 1940 the Court ruled against the Witnesses, but in 1943 they reversed that ruling.

Robert, Tink, and I were separated into different classes. Tink clung to me during lunch hour and recess. Then we joined a long line of girls playing jump rope. I saw Robert wandering around the grounds alone. I knew he was homesick. One day as I was sitting on the ground playing a game of jacks, a small boy rushed up to tell me my brother was fighting.

I knew Robert didn't like to fight. When I came in sight of the scuffle, all I could see was his feet sticking out from under a pile of four or five other boys. He beat his toes against the ground and I was sure his face was buried in the dirt. I screamed, "Let him up! He can't breathe! Let my brother up!" I grabbed a coat collar and pulled one of the boys off and shoved him to the ground. I screamed and clawed until they all backed off. Robert brushed the side of his face.

It was scraped and covered with dirt, and I could see he wasn't face-down after all. By then the principal was headed our way. He took all the boys to his office, including Robert. I wasn't worried about him being in trouble. He could breathe.

After school he told me the principal made them bend over his desk one by one and gave each of them a swat with a big wooden paddle. Then he said to me, "It stung really bad, but don't you tell Mama and Daddy." I never did.

❧

One cold February morning, Mama called up to us to get up and look out the window. "There's a big snow on the ground!" I crawled out from the warm covers and ran barefoot to the window. The view from the balcony of Aunt Dell's Muskogee house had never been this beautiful. Trees in the orchard were draped in white. The lane leading out to the main road was carpeted with snow and the tree limbs were weighted toward the ground. The porch top just below our bedroom window was covered in a fluffy white blanket.

Sid hit the floor and rushed into our room. He pushed on the window, and I helped him lift it. When he tried to push the screen out, I asked him what he was doing.

"I want some snow."

"You can't go out there. You'll fall."

"I just want to get on the roof."

Mama had been building a fire in the cookstove, but then I heard her walking up the stairs. "Where's that cold air comin' from? What are you kids doin' with a window open? My goodness, it's cold as ice up here!" She rushed over, took Sid's arm, and moved him away from the window.

"What are you tryin' to do?"

"Climb out and get some snow."

"You can't climb out there, Sidney Ray. You'll tumble all the way to the ground."

"I've done it before."

"You've what? When?"

"When Robert throwed my cap on the roof."

Mama got down on her knees, looked Sid in the face, and said, "Baby, don't ever do that again. If you fell off that roof, you'd be killed. Do you understand what I'm sayin'?"

Sid nodded his head. "Uh-huh."

"If you wanna play in the snow, get your shoes on and go with Daddy to the barn."

I heard Daddy say as she went downstairs, "That's just like somethin' I'd a done."

Mama said she thought we ought to stay home. The snow looked deep, and it was too cold to walk.

Daddy said we'd do chores and then we'd see. He didn't like for us to miss school.

Sure enough, after breakfast he said he thought we could make it. "It's less than a mile, and I'll walk partway with them."

The sky was gray, and a cold wind blew puffs of snow across the road. Daddy walked with us until we could see the school. The red brick building stood out against the white landscape, but the long building and the outhouses at the edge of the playground were less visible. As Daddy left he told us, "Now don't poke along. Walk fast and you'll stay warmer. I'll come and walk home with you."

We crossed a pasture and a well-beaten path that followed the fence. Skiffs of snow blew across the field, stinging our faces. We waded through snow that came up over the tops of our shoes and my feet felt like chunks of ice. Tink's shoes filled up with snow and she cried. Robert pulled his stocking cap down over his ears and turned his coat collar up, then he helped Tink with her cap and tried to bundle her up. We were all crying. I sat down in the snow to empty my shoes. It was hard to get back up, but Robert kept us moving.

Finally, half frozen, we dragged ourselves into the school yard. Classes started at nine, and we were late. Robert helped Tink into her room and asked her teacher to let her stand by the fire to warm her feet. The teacher took her inside and Robert headed up the wide, winding staircase to his sixth-grade room.

I entered my classroom shivering and crying. Mrs. Woods took a folding chair from the coat closet and sat me by the big potbelly stove. She got down on her knees and took off my wet shoes and socks. "My God, your feet are frozen," she said.

I looked down at my blue feet. My toes were stiff and their tips looked like purple marbles. I wiped tears and said, "But Tink's colder than me." She hugged me and left the room.

Mrs. Woods returned with Tink and Miss Thompson. Two boys left the room and came back with a couple of dishpans filled with snow. I thought the last thing I wanted to do was stick my feet in something cold, but as the women massaged our feet and ankles in the cold wet snow, the blueness faded and circulation returned. We sat by the fire and enjoyed the pampering until we were warm.

At four o'clock, Daddy was there to walk us home. Mrs. Woods told him, "The next time it's this cold, keep them home. A day or two off school won't make that much difference. If that little one had gone another quarter of a mile, I'm afraid she would have frozen to death."

Mama was watching out the window and came to meet us. Daddy had Tink in his arms. "I should a listened to you, Mama. I reckon I didn't know how fast a little one could freeze to death. I knowed it was cold. I just don't know what I was thinkin'!"

We hurried inside and gathered around the fire. Daddy tried again to tell us what school meant to him when he was a little boy, and how bad it hurt him to have to drop out when he was in fifth grade. Then his eyes lit up. "Mama, can we spare a cup of sugar?"

He took us outside and filled a pan with clean packed snow.

Mama skimmed a cup of cream from the milk and poured it into the snow. She added sugar and a spoonful of vanilla. Then she stirred it up and put the lid on. We followed Daddy back outside and buried the pan in the snow.

After the chores were finished and supper was over, we dug the crock out of the snow and Mama scooped the frozen cream with a cup. I savored the sweet vanilla taste and the coarse feeling on my tongue. Daddy and Mama had just treated us to our first homemade ice cream.

All winter in that big house, we tried to keep warm. We had more room than we knew what to do with. There was actually a spare bedroom. Mama and Daddy occupied a big corner bedroom down-stairs. The first room at the top of the stairs was mine and Tink's, and June and Judy slept at the foot of our bed. The hall with a rail-ing guarding the stairs led past Robert and Sid's room. At the end of the hall, a door opened into a long room with a ceiling slanting to the floor on one side. It was on the same level as the other rooms, but it reminded me of Aunt Al's attic. At night Robert pretended the room was haunted. He dared Sid to open the door. Sid slipped along in the dark, but boards creaked and he ran back down the hall, his bare feet pounding against the wood floor. I heard him pounce into bed and scramble for covers, his voice quivering, "Ohh, I'm sooo cold."

"You little coward, you didn't open that door," Robert would say.

"But I touched the doorknob. Bet you won't do that!" And they both laughed and played the game over and over, all winter.

In the spring I picked up the courage to explore the mystery room for myself. The hinges screeched as I pushed the door open. Light came through windows at each end of the room. From the north window I could see the top of Grandpa Gore's barn.

I climbed up on an old wooden trunk beneath the south windowsill. Through the dusty window I saw an orchard yet to be explored. Dropping to my knees, I discovered the rusty latch on the front of the trunk was stuck. I pushed on the round tin piece in the middle of the latch and the sturdy old chest popped open. Under the heavy lid was a pile of worn books. Most of them had leather covers with tattered corners. There were *Treasure Island* and *Kidnapped* by Robert Louis Stevenson, with black-and-white drawings of pirate ships. I saw pirates with black hats and long fierce mustaches, or turbans wrapped around their heads. One walked the deck with a peg leg. They were firing long-barreled pistols or fighting with swords, agony written on their faces as some tumbled into an angry sea.

That evening at supper I said, "I found a trunk full of old books in the haunted room upstairs." And Daddy said, "You leave them books alone; they ain't ours. Don't open that trunk no more."

After that I sneaked into the room whenever I got a chance. If Mama called, I scampered downstairs. I remember her saying, "Was you into them books again? You know what Daddy said." But she never told. That was the beginning of my love for books, and I think Mama knew it was my own treasure island.

An old organ of the Gores sat by itself against one wall in Mama's bedroom. She could get a tune out of it and make it look easy. I spun myself around on the wooden stool. I couldn't reach the pedals but I could stand up, stretch my right leg, and pump with my foot. When I hit the keys with my fingers, out came a strange moaning sound.

Mama said, "Don't play with the organ. It ain't a toy." So I gave up on the groaning old instrument and explored elsewhere.

Early spring found Daddy breaking ground and planting crops. The cornfield was down the hill past the old shack the Montgomerys had lived in for such a little while. Mama weeded. On Saturdays we all worked.

One morning we four older kids followed Daddy to the field. The horses wore their harnesses, and Daddy walked behind them with the reins in both hands. Smoke came from the chimney, and a little black-and-white dog ran out the door. Robert got to his knees and motioned to her. She stopped a few feet from us and wagged her tail.

A voice called, "Here, Geisha! She won't hurt you. She's friendly. She likes people, 'specially kids."

Daddy pulled back on the reins to stop the horses. "How's everything goin', Shorty?"

"Me and Geisha, we're OK. I rounded up enough wood yesterday for a while. I'd like a ride to town sometime, pick up a few things."

Daddy said, "I ride in with Mr. Gore almost every Saturday. I'm sure if you ask, he'll make room for you."

By then Geisha was jumping all over us, going from Robert's arms to each of us. When Robert stood her on the ground, she followed at our heels. Shorty stepped outside the door and called her back.

We questioned Daddy about our new neighbor and he said that he was a hermit, living alone except for the dog.

Robert asked, "How come he's crippled?"

"I don't know why he's so stooped and has to have that cane," Daddy said. "He ain't an old man. You kids stay away from him, you hear me? Shorty seems like a nice guy, but don't go messin' around that old shack no more."

We often saw Shorty wandering in the woods as we rounded up the cows in the evening. Sometimes he was sitting on a tree stump with his cane at his side. He kept his distance, but almost every Saturday he walked up the hill and left Geisha to play with us while he went into town with Daddy and Grandpa Gore.

༆

Daddy bought three cows. Nonie was a roan, sort of gray in color. She wore a bell around her neck. The other two were white-faced Guernseys. In the evening, we listened for the sound of Nonie's bell, knowing the other two would be close by.

Robert, Sid, Tink, and I wandered around the wooded area. We waded in shallow streams and learned to skip rocks. Sid scooped up tadpoles with long tails and watched them flop in his hands. Robert told him, "Let 'em go. They'll turn into frogs." We laughed at him, but he said, "It's true. Their tails come off and they turn into frogs." Sure enough, in a few weeks the tadpoles were gone and little green frogs hopped all over the bank. When we tried to catch them, they jumped in and swam across the stream, kicking both feet as they skimmed the top of the water.

Once in a while one of us found an arrowhead and we all inspected the hard dark flint, skillfully carved by a Native American who occupied those hills long before we appeared on the scene. We hurried home to show Mama.

Robert carried a good pocketknife. Sid could carve wooden horses, cows, pigs, and even dolls. I learned to bury the blade in a log. Robert taught me to hold it by the tip, aim, consider the distance of the log, and get the feel of the knife in my hand. With just the right balance, I learned to toss hard and flip it in the air. It hit the log with a thud, vibrated back and forth a few times, and stayed there.

Robert was now old enough to help Daddy with the morning chores. One morning he rushed back from the barn. "Bessie had the prettiest little calf," he said. "Hurry, Daddy wants you to come and see her."

The baby heifer lay on the floor beside her mother. Her dark reddish coat lay in shiny wet waves. She lifted her white face and stared at us, then pushed up onto her knees and stood up on all four tottery legs as her tiny body swayed up and back.

"My, what a pretty baby calf," Mama said. "What do you reckon we ought to call her?"

"Baby," Tink said. The name stuck.

Daddy usually sold newborn calves, but we kept Baby as a pet. She would grow up and have calves of her own and in time become our best milk cow.

჻

We didn't have to carry water from a well anymore. On the back porch was a pump with a long handle, and water came from the spout. Mama also kept a washtub under the eaves of the house at one corner of the front porch to catch rainwater. She used the fresh soft water to wash our hair.

One day she was fitting a new dress on me when we heard June and Judy screaming. They were playing on the front porch and it wasn't unusual for them to fight over a toy, yelling in a tug-of-war until one won or somebody pulled them apart. We ignored them a while but finally Mama said, "Tink, see what them babies is fightin' over."

A few seconds later, Tink's frantic voice came from the porch. "Mama, June fell in the tub of water!"

Mama pushed me aside and ran out the door. I hurried behind her. Judy was sitting on the edge of the porch pulling on June's arms and screaming at the top of her lungs. June lay on her back in the tub with just her head sticking out. The sight of her sent chills through me as I realized she could have drowned while we ignored her. I was only nine years old, but I was learning how very fragile life is.

Tink lifted June from the tub. Mama took her out, hugged her dripping body, and cried. She kept saying, "June would a drowned if Judy hadn't kept her head above the water."

Tink brought towels and dry clothes for June. Mama dried her off, and wiped her own tears too, all the while thanking God for the safety of her two babies.

57

In the midst of the excitement, Grandpa Gore's car pulled up and Daddy unloaded a long, shallow cardboard box. He set it on the porch and I heard "Peep, peep, peep!" coming from inside. He returned to the car and brought in a few groceries. I lifted the lid of the box and there were a hundred tiny yellow baby chickens. They raised their heads, waddled around in the box, and tried to climb out. We all helped lift them onto the ground where they scurried around and bumped into one another, then spread out over the yard, scratching in the dirt and picking up tiny bits of grain that Daddy tossed down.

A few days later, as June sat in the yard with baby chicks playing all around her, she picked one up by the neck. It kicked and squirmed and when it stopped moving, she set it on the ground and picked up another one. She held on as long as it fought back. By the time Mama discovered her game, half a dozen chicks lay dead on the ground. Looking at a dead animal wasn't a problem for me; it was part of farm life. But when I watched it die, then death seemed cruel.

⌇

One day in early summer, Mama opened a letter from Aunt Addie. Her face lit up as she read the news. "They're comin' to see us. They'll be here in two weeks. Maybe she'll talk Daddy into movin' there."

It was always exciting to talk with Mama about California.

I said, "Daddy always says, 'When the crops is laid by,' don't he, Mama? Maybe Aunt Addie and Uncle Ivan will help us finish our crops and then we can follow them to California. You think they'd do that?"

That got a laugh out of Mama. "No, honey, that's several months away, but Addie can tell him more than she can put in a letter. If they stay a week or so, who knows what might happen. I know Daddy means it when he says 'some day,' but I get so discouraged. Seems like we just put it off one year after another. Now that the Depression is over, Ivan gets lots of work. They bought a house in town with water piped in. Addie has linoleum on all the floors, a bathroom inside, and electricity. They got electric lights in ever' room. Wouldn't it be somethin' just to pull a cord and turn on a light? And not have to carry water or wash clothes on a rubboard no more?"

"How many kids they got now?" I asked.

"There's three boys and three girls. Some of their kids is big now. They'll be here soon and you'll see."

The next two weeks dragged by. Then one day a big black car pulled into the yard. Three teenagers climbed out. Uncle Ivan stepped out tall and straight, wearing a light brown Stetson hat. A plump little woman struggled to open the front door of the car. Her feet dangled as she tried to reach the ground. A pretty, dark-haired toddler slid down from her arms and reached for an older girl who stepped up and took the baby. Daddy rushed out, wrapped his arms around Aunt Addie , and lifted her from the car. Both of them cried. I didn't expect her to be so tiny. She was four feet, eleven inches. At a distance, she looked like one of the kids.

In no time the house was filled with laughing and reminiscing. I felt as if I'd always known them. After a while, we kids ventured upstairs with our cousins. No one was much interested in the old books except Floyd. He was a gangly thirteen-year-old with a mind for literature. He dug around in the trunk and came up with *The Legend of Sleepy Hollow*.

"Ever read this?" he asked. I hadn't, and I asked him what it was about.

"We read it in school last year," he said, and I sat spellbound as he told me about Ichabod Crane and the headless horseman in his own words. Later I sneaked up and gazed at the pictures, remembering the story Floyd had told.

That night, Mama gave the boys' room to Aunt Addie and Uncle Ivan. She carried the kerosene lamp into the next room. Robert, Sid, and Aunt Addie's three boys followed, and she bedded them all down on the floor in the big room at the end of the hall. Sid raced down the hall yelling, "Yeah! We get to sleep in the haunted room!"

Mama laughed and said, "I'm afraid Robert's got him believin' that."

"It is haunted," Sid said. "We hear noises at night, and I seen a ghost."

"You didn't see no ghost," Robert said. "You're afraid to open the door at night."

"I ain't afraid to touch the doorknob. Besides, ghosts come right through the door. I seen 'em. Maybe we'll see one tonight."

After a while, the house quieted down and I heard a noise, something between a moan and the sound of the wind whistling around the corner of the house on a blustery night. "Oh-h-h, who's that sle-e-e-pin' in my-y-y room?" I sat up in bed. A figure in white crept down the hall toward the open door of the big room. It entered the door moaning and Sid screamed. The boys scuffled and fought for covers. The older boys pleaded for the ghost to go away. The house shook with a big roar of laughter. Aunt Addie and Uncle Ivan were laughing, and I could hear Mama and Daddy downstairs laughing too.

The ghost wrestled Sid on the floor. "Get outta my ro-o-om, kid, or I'll wrap you up and roll you down the stairs." Then Sid recognized Floyd as the "ghost" underneath a sheet. Uncle Ivan said, "OK, boys, settle down. Let everyone get some sleep."

❦

For a week the big house rocked with the sound of happy voices. At meal time, we older kids filled our plates and sat on the back porch, while the grownups and babies took places at the dining-room table.

One evening as I sat on the floor with my plate in front of me, I heard Aunt Addie say, "This is a nice house, Bill, but if you moved to California, you could buy a home. You could make seventy-five cents an hour workin' in the fields. That's almost ten dollars a day. You wouldn't believe the cotton they raise there."

"It's hot in the San Joaquin Valley and it don't rain much," Uncle Ivan said, "but they got irrigation. I mean big canals full of water. They run it into the field, then channel it down between the rows. You could work all the time, Bill. You could pick cotton or irrigate or even drive a tractor."

"I don't know if I could drive a tractor," Daddy said.

"You can drive a car, can't you?"

"Well, yeah, but I don't have to worry about keepin' the rows straight when I drive a car." They all laughed, and Daddy said, "We'll get enough money together one of these days. You'll see."

"Aw shucks, Bill," Aunt Addie said. "You keep puttin' it off 'til things get better. You can't wait forever."

"Cotton prices is up. Maybe this fall I can buy a car and we can start savin' for gas money. We'll surprise you."

Mama said, "What we need is a few more cows and chickens. We could save money sellin' cream and eggs."

"Don't wait too long," Aunt Addie said. "Your family's growin' up pretty fast."

The week flew by and we said our good-byes. We hugged and then cried as Aunt Addie, Uncle Ivan, and the kids got in their big black 1936 Chevrolet and drove away. The kids waved from the back window of the car. It disappeared through the trees.

ᒍ

The rains came that year and, for a while, the crops flourished. One afternoon the sky grew dark and wind blew. We stood on the front porch with Daddy and watched a funnel cloud dip to the ground and hit the little town of Pryor about ten miles away. Mama was frantic. A few minutes later the rain poured.

Healthy green leaves and colorful pink blossoms covered the cotton stalks. As the blossoms dropped off, little green cotton bolls appeared. Where the plants had not survived, there were long skips in the rows, but crops were like that every year. Daddy said, "It looks like we'll have a good cash crop this year."

Then an army of boll weevils moved in. They entered at the far end of the field and worked their way through, stripping the stalks clean. Grandpa Gore came over to inspect the situation. Daddy said, "I wonder if we could drive 'em out."

"There's too many. They'd just come right back. Besides, they're everywhere this year. I ain't ever seen so many before. I'll go into town and get a spray or somethin'."

They tried poisonous dusting powder, but they didn't have the necessary equipment to spread it across a large area, and the weevils continued to move slowly across the field. I sat upstairs with my books, looking out the window. I was too young to realize what was happening, but I could see the weevils cutting a wider swath through the field. At the far end, behind them, the stalks were brown and bare, stripped clean. Ahead was lush green foliage, but the pesky creatures were working their way through it, closer and closer to the house.

The boll weevils destroyed every stalk. Farmers for miles around lost cotton crops that year. The cash crop was gone, but we still had the cows and chickens and enough new potatoes spread on the floor of the storage shed to last several months. That, with Mama's canned fruit and vegetables, would help us through winter. When the corn and headed feed was stored in the barn, Daddy took work wherever he could find it.

᷍

In the spring, Daddy debated about whether to plant cotton again, and in the end he decided on corn and feed. Then Henry Gore talked him into helping with a large cotton patch about a mile away along Route 66. Daddy planted crops for himself and Grandpa Gore and entered a partnership with Henry. The crops got off to a good start as we were winding down our second year of school at Sequoyah.

Sunday, May 10, was Mother's Day. Daddy walked Tink and me through the trees to spend the day at Grandma Gore's. We only knew her as the lady in Grandpa Gore's car. She always smiled and waved at us when they picked Daddy up. We felt better when we learned that her granddaughter, Emma, would be there, too.

The three of us played all day with paper dolls and coloring books. We knew nothing about the arrival of a new baby until Daddy came for us. We hurried home to see a beautiful baby sister in Mama's arms. Her name was Peggy Sue, but to us she would always be Susie.

For two years the twins had been "the babies," but now there were three. Susie fit right into the picture. Long after we were all grown, Sid still referred to June, Judy, and Susie as "the babies."

The summer after Susie was born, another of Daddy's sisters, Aunt Ada, came with her family from California. Uncle Leonard surprised us when he started looking for a place for them to live near us.

Daddy said, "I thought California was the Garden of Eden."

"Well, it ain't," Uncle Leonard said. "There's lots of poor folks. Ada and me, we lived in labor camps, and we done everything from climbin' ladders and pickin' fruit to pullin' a cotton sack. Even cut grapes, and I swear, we just couldn't get ahead. So we come back home. You try it if you want, Bill, but it ain't everything folks say."

His remarks set me back on my heels. I just knew Daddy would give up the idea of moving, but to my surprise, when I asked Mama, she said, "No, Daddy don't put much stock in what Leonard says. And Ada, she told me she didn't want to move back here. She had to go along with it. She said, 'One of these days, he will go back to California. He's just a restless soul.'"

That Saturday, Daddy rode into town with Uncle Leonard and

came back in the late afternoon. Twelve-year-old Ezra stood in the yard watching as his dad walked loop-legged across the driveway, his eyes glassy, a half-pint whiskey bottle in his shirt pocket. Uncle Leonard staggered, grabbed for the gatepost, and fell into the yard. Ezra dropped his head and walked around the house out of sight.

Uncle Leonard's drinking problem was not a surprise to my parents. It disturbed Daddy, but Mama said it was up to Ada to decide what to do, because she loved him, and Aunt Ada stayed.

↶

Ezra had been a year old when Aunt Ada and Uncle Leonard moved to California during the Dust Bowl era. They returned with three girls and three boys, and the week of their arrival stands out as one of the most fun weeks of my childhood. The orchard became a playground as we played kick the can, hide-and-seek, and other games. We climbed the tall mulberry tree in the middle of the orchard. It was loaded with long dark berries, almost black, and sweet and juicy. We picked the tasty fruit by the handfuls. The best berries were the ones that had fallen to the ground.

Sheep sorrel grew wild around the trunks of the trees and small bushes in the back of the orchard. The coarse weedy plants, with their tangy leaves, were sometimes used to make wine and to add a sharp lemony taste to pies. One day I was on my knees picking and eating the tasty leaves. I reached in closer to the base of the trees, then jerked my hand away instinctively, scooting my body a safe distance from what turned out to be a coiled copperhead snake. Coppery red bands between chestnut red ones circled its broad body. I called for Robert, and all the kids ran toward me. I caught Sid and held him back.

"Let me go! I want to see!" he said.

"He'll bite you," I said, "and he could kill you." But when he begged me, I let him take my hand and get a little closer. Robert and Ezra kept the other small children at a safe distance. They threw rocks at the snake, causing him to curl up like a rope. He squirmed and hissed. When Sid tried to get closer, Robert yelled at him that the snake was trying to fight us. He told Sid, "See that big rock? Help Betty bring it to me."

Sid pulled away from me and ran toward the rock, but our ten-year-old cousin Almus reached it first. He walked over and threw the rock and pinned the snake under it. "Now he can't fight back!"

The boys killed the snake and pulled the flat limp body from under the tree. They draped the three-foot carcass across a stick and carried it down through the orchard toward the house, Sid yelling at Mama to look at what we had.

Mama and Aunt Ada came out, and Mama gasped and covered her mouth. "Oh, dear God. It's a copperhead, ain't it?"

"Yeah, and we killed him!" Robert said. "Betty almost put her hand on him."

Mama wanted to know everything. I told her how I was picking sheep sorrel and how I had no idea the snake was there. Aunt Ada was on the porch. She said, "Betty's lucky. A rattlesnake'll warn you, but copperheads, they just lay there quiet, 'til a person gets too close, and then they strike."

"Do they kill you?" I asked.

"Not many grown-ups die, but kids do," she said. She and Mama agreed we should play closer to the house. Mama told Robert, "Get rid of him. Bury him or take him away and throw him in the brush. Hurry! Get him outta sight and away from the little kids."

She told us it was time to bring the cows in. That was something we all liked to do. We played in the woods and searched for arrowheads as we listened for Nonie's bell. That summer Sid learned to ride saplings to the ground. The tall, spindly, flexible trees were not easy to climb. The weight of our bodies caused the limbs to bend slowly as we hung on tight, riding back to the ground. Sid was small and wiry and he could climb higher than anyone before the tree bent.

Then he clung tight as the trunk weaved and headed down. He let go and lay on the ground rolling and laughing while the tree popped back up into the air and swayed a few times before settling. He climbed up and down again until Robert made him give it up.

After two weeks, Aunt Ada and Uncle Leonard moved to a farm near Wagoner, where Uncle Leonard had family. We had grown to love our cousins and we missed them, but they were close enough to visit sometimes.

⤵

In the fall, when the patch of cotton along Route 66 was ready to pick, Grandma and Grandpa Bristol paid us a visit and Grandpa helped in the field.

Henry's family lived in a big white two-story house behind the general store. The cotton field started right beside the store.

On Saturdays, Robert picked cotton with Mama and Daddy. Tink and I stayed home and helped Grandma with housework and the babies. One evening Mama said to Grandma, "The funniest thing happened today. We saw a long, black car drive down the highway. It passed the cotton field and then turned around and come back and parked. Two well-dressed women got out and walked down through the field in high-heeled shoes and nice, two-piece suits. One wore a cute little black hat."

Grandma laughed and said, "What in the world did they want?"

"Well," Mama said, "they was travelin' across the country, and they never seen cotton before. One of them said, 'I wonder if you folks would let us pick some cotton, and take a few pictures?'

"Daddy said, 'Sure,' and he pulled the strap off his shoulder and gave it to one of the women. The lady pulled the sack on over her hat, swung it over her shoulder, and said, 'Do I have it on right?' Then she picked a few stalks of cotton, pulling that heavy load along behind her and wearin' them high heels while her friend took pictures. She took some pictures of us too.

"They took our address and said they'd mail us some of the pictures."

And that is how I happen to have pictures of my parents and Robert and my Grandpa Bristol, and of a woman whose name no one remembers, picking cotton along Route 66 near Claremore, Oklahoma, in 1943.

❧

Henry Gore didn't pick cotton. He drove his pickup into the field, chatted a while, gave out a few orders, and left. One evening that fall, as we sat around the supper table, Grandpa Bristol asked, in his usual loud voice, "Bill, what do you think about that offer Henry made today? River bottom land is real rich soil, you know."

"I know," Daddy said. "We could sure use a good bumper crop."

"I like it here," Mama said. "The kids is happy and Grandpa Gore is a good old man. He likes Bill. We get by real good."

"But, Elsie, Henry says there's two good houses and the one we would live in is the newest and best. It sets back off the road. The houses and barns are up on a hill, and the farmland lays down along the Verdigris River. I think we ought to at least look at it."

Grandpa thought Mama should go with Daddy to look at it. Grandma said, "Comes a time when a woman wants to get settled." She knew Mama was happy where we were. But in the end, Mama said it wouldn't hurt to go look.

They returned late in the day and Mama said it was a nice house. Daddy had told Henry he'd talk to Grandpa Gore and think it over. Everybody was talking about what it would take to get enough money to go to California.

The next thing Mama knew, she was packing and getting ready to move again.

South Limestone

FIRST WE PASSED THE SCHOOL. It sat a few yards back of the edge of the road. There was a playground with equipment and a small baseball diamond, but we were sad to have left Sequoyah's school and Grandpa Gore's big house. Daddy kept telling us it was all for the better. "With rich land like that, you just can't hardly lose." He was anxious to plant a crop in the river bottom.

A quarter mile past the school we entered the ranch, drove past the main house, and circled the barn. We followed a dirt road across the top of the hill to the end of the land. There stood a big white house with a porch across the front. It was built on a hillside overlooking the Verdigris River, so the porch was on stilts about four feet off the ground, and I visualized playing beneath it on hot days, in the cool shade.

As soon as we stopped, I ran toward a long flight of steps, but Mama called me back to help with the babies. On the porch, we stopped to look out over the treetops. Beyond lay lush fields, ready for Daddy's horses and plow. In the distance, trees lined the banks of the river. Here and there a break in the trees exposed the water as the river wound like a snake across the green landscape.

At the edge of the backyard, a couple of T-shaped wooden poles supported four clotheslines, and just beyond the yard there was a round silo begging to be explored. I got on my hands and knees to peek through a small opening at the bottom. In record time, we had crawled into the empty silo and turned it into a playhouse.

Later that first day, Tink discovered a box of old high-heeled shoes, all size five, in the corner of a bedroom. We pranced through the house, changing shoes every few minutes, until Mama grew tired of the noise and said, "Them shoes is gettin' on my nerves. If you're gonna clomp around, go outside."

There was another long porch down the side of the house and a small one off the kitchen. About twenty feet out, a platform encased the well, standing high enough to keep kids off it. I noticed new, unpainted boards behind the wood cookstove, and a portion of the floor that had been replaced. When I asked Mama about it, she said that the woman who had lived there before us had tried to light a fire with wet wood. When she couldn't get it started with crumbled paper and kindling, she'd gotten a can of kerosene and dashed it on the papers. Flames had leaped into the can and it exploded. Her clothes caught fire. She ran into the yard and nearly burned to death.

"Was she alone?" I asked.

"No," Mama said, "her family was here, and the neighbors run across the field. They was able to save her, but she was left with scars over most of her body. It's a wonder the house didn't burn to the ground."

The family who owned the ranch lived in Tulsa about fifteen miles away. They had two teenage daughters who came out on weekends to go horseback riding. I watched them with envy as they raced around the pasture. Mama had seen her cousin thrown and dragged to death, his foot caught in a stirrup, so it was no surprise she seldom let Tink and me near a horse.

⌇

I spent the remainder of that school year in a state of fear. The older boys in school fought and carried knives, and more than once somebody got a shirt slashed. One time they backed Robert against the swings and knifed him through his shirt, drawing blood. Fistfights and bloody noses were common. Our teacher couldn't control the situation. The rowdy boys called her "Old Lady Lawrence." They blew spit wads and hit her in the face. She kept them after school, but they just waited for a chance to crawl out the door and catch up with the rest of us as we walked down the road toward home.

One day at dismissal, Miss Lawrence discovered her keys were missing. Her ride, Mr. Bridges, was waiting out by the road for her and his two kids. She stuck her head out the door and waved and said, "Yoohoo, be there in a minute." The boys roared "Yoohoo! Yoohoo!" and everyone from first to eighth grade laughed. The more she stomped up and down the aisle pleading for her keys, the worse those boys sneered. I had never seen her so mad.

A boy we called Spud hopped around making noises like a monkey. By the time Miss Lawrence reached him, her face was red as fire. She backhanded him across the face and he staggered, grabbed the side of the desk, regained his balance, and then headed toward her with his fists clenched. He swung at her, but she was out of reach. She picked up a child's chair and threw it at him. He ducked and the chair hit Robert.

The other boys caught Spud and pleaded with him, "Stop it. We'll all be expelled."

She said, "You're already expelled for the rest of this year, or I'm leavin'. I won't put up with this any longer."

It seemed like an hour passed as Miss Lawrence kept going to the door and calling to Mr. Bridges. Finally someone sneaked the keys onto her desk and the day ended.

On the way home, Spud said, "Do you reckon Old Lady Lawrence will be back?" In fact, we never saw her again. A young woman with a son in first grade took her place. The word was that Miss Lawrence was hospitalized.

༉

Later that spring, Daddy rode into town with Henry Gore to buy groceries. While he was there, he noticed an old brown Chevy parked in back of a service station and asked if it was for sale. The owner said, "It don't want to start no more." He offered it for almost nothing and Daddy paid him, put a dollar's worth of gas in it, and Henry and some other men pushed it until the engine kicked on. Daddy drove home and parked on a slope. He left the car in gear so it wouldn't roll. When he got ready to start the car, he took it out of gear and let it roll down. Sometimes the whole family got behind and pushed. After it got up a little speed, Daddy jumped in, pushed the clutch in, and put it in gear. Then when he let out on the clutch it almost always started. We got a lot of miles out of that old Chevrolet.

Daddy planted cotton, corn, and feed in the rich soil between the house and the river. The crops sprouted. As they grew, we kids would weed after school and on Saturdays. Then the rains came. At first they were a welcome sight, but after several days of heavy rain, my parents became restless. The sky grew dark, and as Mama watched for funnel clouds, Daddy worried about the crops, saying, "If this keeps up, that river'll come out of its banks and take everything we've worked for."

Our grandparents came to visit, and one stormy afternoon, Mama and Grandma Bristol gathered us all into the living room. Daddy stood on the front porch clinging to one of the pillars as the wind howled and whipped across the porch. Trees on the hillside bent and swayed. Dead branches broke off, then flew a few yards and shattered as they hit the ground.

Mama opened the door and pleaded, "Daddy, help me get the kids into the cellar."

He called to her above the noise of the storm. "We don't need to go to the cellar. It's just high winds. Keep the kids in the house. We ain't never been in the path of a tornado. You worry too much about the wind."

Grandma said, "When that cyclone hit Wagner, Poppie and me was there. People was killed, and it tore that town to pieces."

"Daddy, please," Mama said, "I can't get the kids all down the hill by myself."

Daddy told her again not to take us to the cellar, to go back in and close the door before she got sucked out onto the porch. "It'll blow you down if you step out here," he said. But Mama wouldn't stop pleading, so he finally let go of the pillar. His hat almost blew off his head and he grabbed it with both hands. His shirt and overalls sucked tight against his skin and he struggled with every step against the wind's force.

Finally he stepped safely inside, and there was a loud crash as a big tree in the backyard fell to the ground. Mama and Grandma screamed and huddled us all together like a couple of mother hens. Then they rushed us out the door. Grandpa, who was almost deaf, had been looking on. He knew something was wrong, so he grabbed Sid's hand and followed us. We all clung together crossing the porch, and we fought our way down the steps and across the driveway.

The cellar was dug into the hillside a few yards down from the house. Robert lifted the latch and the door swung back and crashed tight against the outside wall. We crowded through. Mama handed Susie to Grandma and went back after Daddy, even though Grandma begged her not to. Robert and Grandpa pried the door loose and it sucked shut.

A few minutes later, Mama dragged Daddy into the cellar. All of us crouched together in the dark, damp, musty-smelling hole in the side of the hill. The door rattled and banged.

Mama called, "Betty, where are you?"

"Here, Mama."

"Is June and Judy with you?"

"Judy's here, and Tinkie's got June."

"Where are you, Sid?"

Daddy said, "He's settin' on my knee. Now stop worryin'. Everybody's safe. We'll stay here 'til it dies down. But it ain't no tornado. You'll see. It's just a strong wind."

And he was right. Before long I heard big drops of rain pounding against the cellar door. Robert unlatched the door, and we ran back to the house in a downpour. The only damage from the wind was the mess of the fallen tree.

〜

Then there was the rain. The river came out of its banks and across the bottomland. Each day it grew wider and crept farther up the hill. We were on high ground, but other people weren't as lucky. From the porch I watched the flood waters carry a house away with only the roof showing above the water.

When at last the rains stopped and the water subsided, we went scavenger hunting. Everything from old bottles and cans to broken pieces of furniture had washed down the river and clung to the trunks of trees on the side of the hill. But the crops were gone and it was too late to plant again. Mama cried and said, "Henry's all talk. We ought to have stayed with Grandpa Gore."

Daddy said, "We can stay here the rest of the year. That's the deal."

A neighbor man got Daddy a part-time job at a grain elevator in Claremore that sat beside the railroad tracks. He unloaded hundred-pound sacks of feed and grain from boxcars and delivered them to feed stores. We lived in the big white house for the rest of that year.

Grandpa Bristol borrowed a drift boat and went fishing in the river. Late one evening, Mama sent Tink and me to look for him and we found him just as he was getting out of the boat. We waded out to climb in while he pulled the boat ashore and tied it up, but when we neared the boat, we saw two black eels about three feet long and a couple inches in diameter. They wiggled and squirmed all over the bottom of the boat. Grandpa laughed as we jumped backward, nearly sitting in the water.

"Ain't you never seen a eel before?" he said. "They won't hurt you. They're just a fish. Your mommie seen me catch lots of eels. I bet she'll cook 'em for supper too." And just to please Grandpa, she did. He skinned them, and Mama rolled the pieces in flour and meal and fried them, but she fussed all through supper, afraid one of us kids would choke on a tiny bone.

⌇

My grandparents returned home. The war raged on, and one by one Mama's family migrated to California. They settled in the San Francisco Bay area and worked in the shipyards. Finally Grandma and Grandpa Bristol sold what they owned, too, and bought one-way tickets to Pittsburg, California.

They stopped to see us before they left. I went with Daddy into Claremore to meet them. We stood on the platform as a long locomotive came into sight. Young men in army uniforms were hanging out every window. I stood close to Daddy as they made their way into the terminal for a rest stop. I had heard a lot about the war, but this was the first of many troop trains to pass through and leave their impression on my young life.

Our grandparents stepped off the train, each carrying a large cardboard suitcase. Grandpa set his on the ground and shook Daddy's hand, then reached in his back pocket. "Mommie, did I give you my wallet?" he said in a trembling voice.

"No, Poppie. I ain't got your wallet."

"Check your pocketbook, Mom. If you ain't got my wallet, it's gone!"

Grandma fumbled through her purse. She had the tickets, but she said Grandpa had kept his wallet. It had every dime they had in it, and it was gone.

Daddy couldn't believe it. He said maybe Grandpa had dropped it. I had never seen my grandpa cry, but as we all hurried back toward the boxcar, he sobbed, "Mommie, ask the conductor if we can go back on the train and look."

Daddy and I climbed the steps and followed them. We went up and down the aisle, looking under seats and between seats, anywhere a wallet could be, but it wasn't anywhere to be found. The conductor helped us. He shook his head and said, "I see this happen more and more. A pickpocket probably spotted you the minute you stepped on the train."

Grandpa cried all the way home. He couldn't eat supper. The next morning Mama had a hard time getting him to eat breakfast. He walked the yard, grieving. Grandma kept reminding him that she had their tickets. "We'll just get on the train and make that four-day ride just the way we planned. Elmer'll meet us in Pittsburg. We'll both get jobs in the shipyards, and we'll be OK. You'll see, Poppie. You'll see." That's exactly what they did; it was the only choice they had.

⌇

We celebrated the holiday season at South Limestone. The radio played Bing Crosby's "I'm Dreaming of a White Christmas." We learned all the words and everyone sang it at school.

There was no prize at the pie supper that year, but if there had been, surely I would have won. My banana cream pie was concealed in a red, white, and blue box. Mama had covered the box with white crepe paper, then placed a blue patch with tiny white stars in the upper left-hand corner. She cut strips of red and glued them on with white between each one. A little red ruffle bordered the flag all the way around the top of the box. The crowd gasped as the auctioneer raised my pie box and tilted it slightly. At that time, I took my mother's artistic ability for granted. She was Mama. She could make something out of nothing. She could do anything.

As the year came to a close, Henry Gore decided to stay and take another chance on the bottomland, but Daddy said, "I ain't gonna gamble away another year's work. I don't know for sure where we'll move to, but we can't stay here."

I listened anxiously as my parents again debated a move to California. By now I knew all the arguments. One of our closest neighbors had just sold out and gone. I said, "If the Koffman's can afford to leave, how come we can't?"

Daddy said, "Because it takes money to make a trip like that. They sold their farm. We ain't got a farm to sell, and if we did have one, I ain't sure I'd sell it."

"But we got a car," I said. "All we need is money for gas."

He laughed. "That old brown Chevy barely makes it into Claremore and back, and sometimes it don't. No, baby, we can't go this year. I seen a place for sale over by Grandpa Gore. He said them folks might rent it to us for a year. I think we can raise a good patch of cotton there."

Robert yelled, "Yeah!" and Tink and I joined in. We were going back to Sequoyah.

Return to Sequoyah

I WAS HAPPY TO BE BACK in Sequoyah school with a wonderful teacher, Miss Woods. She assigned us projects and activities that made me love learning. Route 66 was about a quarter mile from our house. Troop trains dashed through like speeding bullets, with soldiers waving from every window. Long freight trains loaded with army trucks, tanks, and jeeps brought the war closer than ever. Young men from the area were gone, reminding us of the terrible sacrifices that were being made.

The general store sat across the highway from the railroad tracks. One day as Tink and I hurried out to check the mail and wave to the soldiers on the passing midday troop train, we saw a small crowd gathered in front of the store. The passenger train whistled in the distance, and we noticed Annie Gardner with her three little boys in front of the crowd. The oldest boy was jumping up and down and yelling, "There it comes, Mama! There it comes!" He placed his arm around his younger brother's shoulder and said, "Remember to watch for a white hankie, Tommy."

The long silver train came into sight at its usual fast speed. Soldiers' arms were hanging out of every window. Several cars passed and then everyone seemed to yell at once. "There he is, Annie!"

I looked where the crowd was pointing. A lone soldier leaned his head and shoulders out the window. His arms stretched far beyond anyone else's, and he waved a white handkerchief.

"It's Daddy! There's Daddy! Daddy!" the two older boys cried as they jumped and waved both hands. The crowd stood back, arms waving in the air as one of our local heroes passed through. Annie held her two-year-old in her arms. She cried and pointed to her husband, and then, just that fast, the train disappeared into the distance.

Tink and I wiped our tears as the crowd quietly broke up and people drifted inside.

At night, I often lay with my face in the upstairs window and watched trains passing through. The long locomotives were lit from engine to caboose as they glided across the countryside. Their headlights beamed, lighting the tracks ahead. I listened to the mournful whistles and I thought of "The Cannonball Express," the song Daddy liked to sing along with Ernest Tubbs and the Grand Ole Opry on Saturday nights, about the train moving through so fast. I loved the whistle's lonesome sound as the train traveled through the night.

We hadn't been able to go back to Grandpa Gore's house because it was occupied, so we rented another farm. The new house wasn't far from the old one. It was two stories with wood floors and a long stone porch. Mama planted zinnias along the porch.

When we first moved into that old house, we fought bedbugs. They laid their eggs in the small places around the buttons of the mattresses. First we tried to kill them with kerosene. Mama, Tink, and I sprayed around the buttons with a hand sprayer, and we dipped rags in kerosene and squeezed it onto the eggs. We smashed them too. We did everything but burn the house down. Mama cried, but our work was in vain.

Then Mama heard about a new insecticide called D.D.T. that the U.S. Army had used in Naples to halt a typhus epidemic. She read that it was being used on livestock for lice, and also to get rid of termites and bedbugs, so she bought a can, without a thought to what it might do to us. The bedbugs disappeared without a trace.

In the field, Daddy's plow turned up rich dark soil, because the land had not been farmed for a few years. Tink, Sid, and I followed behind Daddy, enjoying the feeling of the cool earth as we burst clods with our bare feet. During harvest season, Daddy helped neighboring farmers thresh wheat and bale hay. Women gathered to cook the noon meal at Ryder's farm. Tink and I went along and spent the day with their daughters.

White workers ate at a large wooden table in the spacious dining room. Black workers waited at the back door for plates of food to be handed to them, then they sat on the steps or in the shade of a tree. Years later, when the events of the sixties caused us all to look back, I asked Daddy how he had felt about all that, and he said, "That's just the way it was in them days. Nobody questioned it."

In exchange for the men's help, Mr. Ryder loaned them his equipment, and the farmers moved from field to field until all the crops were harvested.

One Sunday morning, threatening black clouds rolled in and Daddy left early to help bale hay. I was worried, but Daddy said, "What's a man to do? If I don't work today, the fresh-mowed hay will get wet and mold. We'll lose it all."

Daddy had been known to walk out to his fields to avoid a Sunday picnic, but this was the first time I could remember him ever really working on a Sunday. The Sabbath was a day he attended church and then rested. It was a sin to work. I was afraid my daddy would go to hell.

The cotton crop Daddy raised that year was the envy of other farmers, and the farm was sold. He asked to stay on another year, thinking then we'd have enough money to go to California. Artie Morris, who bought the farm, wanted a share of the crop and Daddy agreed, rather than move again so soon. He raised corn and cotton, still working part-time at the grain elevator in Claremore. He was able to trade in the old brown Chevy and pay the difference for a little red Model A pickup.

We loved our tiny truck, with its short bed for hauling. We put the tailgate down and rode with our feet dangling out the back. Sometimes, though, Daddy didn't have money for gas, and he hitchhiked into town. He almost always got a ride right away.

One evening he was late getting home, and before long, Mama was in a panic. She sent Robert and Sid to look for him. They came back without him. It was getting dark by then and she cried and wrung her hands.

"What if he got in the car with someone he didn't know? He trusts everybody. Maybe they knocked him in the head and robbed him. He could be layin' in a ditch somewhere. We could never find him."

"Mama," Robert said. "If no one picked him up, he's gotta walk six miles. There ain't many cars on the road this time of day."

Mama couldn't just wait. She said, "Come on. We'll walk, and if you're right, we'll meet him someplace."

Mama and Robert disappeared into the night. For a long time I could hear her calling Daddy's name. Finally it stopped. I thought it was because she was out of hearing distance, but they had met Daddy just before he turned off the highway. As Robert said, he had walked six miles, after lifting hundred-pound sacks of grain all day.

It's no wonder Mama worried. Daddy was sick a lot. He had severe headaches. She tried everything from hot packs and cold packs to prayer, but nothing took away the pain. It just had to run its course. His mother had suffered from bad headaches for several months before she died; Daddy was nine years old. Then there were mornings when his stomach was settled sore and he couldn't stand up straight for the pain. Mama would motion us to be quiet, saying, "Daddy had another cramping spell last night." After many years of suffering, it turned out to be gallbladder attacks. When Daddy was eighteen, his father had died of stomach cancer. At the time, there was no way of knowing what caused Daddy's suffering.

꜠

Then came the day Mama had feared since the war began. A notice arrived from the draft board, addressed to Bill Grant. Mama opened it, and sure enough, Daddy had been classified 1-A.

She started watching the road long before Daddy got home. When at last the little red pickup came into sight, she went into the yard to wait. As though she couldn't find the words, she handed Daddy the card through the window of the car. He looked at it and then climbed out.

She said, "Daddy, we got seven kids. Surely they wouldn't draft you, would they? Archie Ryder got deferred to help his Daddy farm."

"I don't know, Mama. All I can do is go to the draft board tomorrow. Try not to worry."

At supper, Daddy said, "You know, Mama, if it wasn't for leavin' you and the kids, I might enjoy seein' the world."

"You mean you'd like to go?"

"No. But if I didn't have a family, I wouldn't worry about it. I don't want to leave you and the kids. You know that. I don't know what I'd do if they took me and I had to leave you. I can't believe they'd do that. But I don't know. I just don't know."

That night I closed my eyes and thought of ways I could help Mama keep us together. Maybe she could ride the bus into Tulsa and work at the defense plant with our neighbor, Zelda. I'd stay home from school and take care of the little kids. Maybe Tink and I could take turns. Or maybe we would go to California. I fell asleep and dreamed I was trying to find Daddy. Someone told me he got out of the army and came home and couldn't find us. I woke up crying.

The next day, they went to the draft board. I guess Mama thought if they decided to take Daddy, she could talk them out of it. As it turned out, Daddy had just turned thirty-six, and they only drafted men through age thirty-five. He was safe, but it had nothing to do with how many of us kids there were.

꒐

Archie Ryder was the youngest of three sons. The Ryder farm adjoined ours. The oldest brother, Sam, had been wounded in action. He returned home with a Purple Heart, a medal with the head of George Washington on it, hanging on a purple silk ribbon. The third boy, Ross, was reported missing in action, and for several months the Ryders didn't know if he was dead or alive. Eventually they learned he was in a German prison camp, where he remained for almost three years, returning to Sequoyah in May 1945, soon after Germany's surrender.

In the Pacific, war waged on and troop trains and war materials kept coming through Sequoyah. Then, late one summer afternoon, as I was sitting with my feet hanging from the barn loft window, watching the traffic on Route 66, a Greyhound bus pulled in and stopped at the general store. A few minutes later, a young man in a navy uniform left the store, walked past the Ryder place, and headed across the meadow toward our house. Mama stepped out the front door and called me to help bring in dry laundry.

I pointed across the meadow and said, "Is that James? That man who just got off the bus?"

She looked up and threw the clothes she had in her arms onto the steps and ran to meet him. James was our cousin, the boy Grandma Bristol had raised because his own mother died soon after he was born. I remembered him having fun and making mischief, and then one day Mama said he had joined the navy. She had been upset, saying, "He's a kid. He's too young to go to war." She worried about him all the time. She would say, "I wonder how James is today." Or, "I just know he's homesick." Or, "Thank God, he's not a combat soldier."

He was a Navy Seabee, assigned to a construction battalion. He was home on furlough and he had come to see us before shipping out to Japan. That night at dinner he told us that Aunt Dell and Uncle

Ewell had sold their house in Muskogee and that Aunt Dell and the girls were leaving for California the next week by train.

"She wants you to come and see her."

Mama asked, "Why ain't Ewell goin' too?"

"He's gonna stay and work for a few more weeks. They don't have to be out for a month, so he said he might as well work a while longer. He's got family in Los Angeles. Aunt Dell and the girls are going there. Can you come to Muskogee for a couple days?"

Mama looked at Daddy, who said, "We'll see."

～

Daddy took us to Claremore, where we boarded the train. Mama, Susie, James, the twins, and I all got on. The babies rode for free and sat on our laps. I sat beside James the whole way and was proud of him in his navy uniform. He talked to Mama across the aisle. I stood Judy between me and the window so that she could watch the tall prairie grass blowing in the breeze. When another train dashed by on the next track, she sat down hard on my lap, and James laughed.

The train station in Muskogee was swarming with military men from the army base nearby. Uncle Ewell met us dressed in his plumber's coveralls.

We helped Aunt Dell clean out the house and pack for the trip to California. She gave all her leftover material to Mama, and Mama was in heaven. I don't think it occurred to me that I was standing on the upstairs balcony for the last time.

Mama and Aunt Dell reminisced, and then they got around to the question of whether Daddy would ever leave Oklahoma. Mama said he would, when we had enough money. She was feeding a wet towel through the wringer of Aunt Dell's Maytag washing machine, and she said, "Maybe we'll have electricity in California and I can get a washer like this."

Aunt Dell said, "Elsie, why don't you go into town and do your laundry in one of them Laundromats? It only cost a dime a load."

Mama hadn't known it cost so little. We could go in when Daddy went to work.

That was the end of building a fire under an iron kettle in the backyard to heat water, the end of bending over to scrub garments on a washboard. All that was left to do was hang them on the line when we got home. And it meant I got to go to town almost every week.

Before we left for town, we sorted the clothes. After the wash, white clothes would go into bleach water before rinsing. With colored clothes, Mama fed them through the ringer and I caught them and lifted them above the bleach solution and into the rinse water. I had a habit of daydreaming, and once in a while a colored garment almost touched the bleach water, but Mama was always watching. "Pay attention, Betty," she would say. "Get your head outta that sack."

If Daddy had to work all day on Saturday, Mama and I left the wet laundry in the car for him to bring home and we rode the Greyhound bus back the six miles to Sequoyah and got off in front of Mrs. Morris's store. One day as we waited in the Claremore bus depot, a shabbily dressed man came out of the restroom fumbling with the buttons of his sweater. He staggered toward me and Mama and sat down heavily in the seat beside me. Mama motioned me to the other side of her, but before I could move, the man leaned over, blew his breath in my face, and said in a loud voice, "They said the president died. Said it on the radio."

With shock and disbelief, Mama said, "Are you sure? Where did you hear it?"

"It's so, ma'am. I heared it across the street at the barber shop on the radio. They said President Roosevelt had a stroke or something. He's dead." He started to cry and talk about what a fine man Mr. Roosevelt was. Mama was wiping tears as our bus pulled in. I wanted to tell the man I was sorry, but Mama pulled me out the door.

She talked and cried on the way home. "I don't know what we're gonna do with the war and all. Seems like the whole world depends on President Roosevelt. We need him to get us outta the war in Japan. And he's done a lot for our country. We was in a awful shape when he took office. Mr. Roosevelt brought us outta the Depression."

I asked, "Who'll be president now?"

She said, "Mr. Truman, I reckon. I don't know much about him. I don't see how anyone can fill Franklin Roosevelt's shoes."

That evening, Daddy came home sad and told Mama, "You know that guy Glasser, who works at the grain elevator? He had the nerve to say, 'That S.O.B. won't run again now.' I don't know how a workin' man can talk like that."

A black cloud fell over the country for days. It was all people talked about at school, at the store, on the radio. I was twelve years old, and Roosevelt was the only president I knew. I'd worn a Roosevelt-Truman button to school for months during his last campaign and never gave a thought that he wouldn't win. I knew Mama and Daddy were voting for him.

Now he was dead.

Then in late summer, everyone listened intently to the radio for the latest war news. It seemed to me we had always been at war. One day Daddy sent Tink and me to the store to buy a newspaper. Mr. Ryder was in the yard and he called to us. "Hey, girls, could I see the headlines?"

He unfolded the paper and read aloud, "War ends in the Pacific. Japanese surrender." For the next few days all we heard about on the radio was our secret weapon, the powerful bomb our country had dropped on Japan. No one else knew how to make it. Now President Truman was a hero after all.

༄

As summer came to a close, we sat on the front steps in the evenings and watched fireflies flickering just after dark. Sometimes we caught them in fruit jars, watching their lights come and go against the side of the jar as they tried to escape. Then at bedtime we opened the jars and traced their lights as they blinked across the yard and disappeared into the darkness.

I entered eighth grade in September. I was getting to be a young lady. One day, Mama showed me a drawer full of baby clothes. There were tiny shoes made from Daddy's old felt Stetson hat, with little pink roses embroidered on the toes. She had a stack of white flannel gowns and cotton batiste dresses with the same tiny roses, her trademark. She told me she was expecting another baby in December, and she asked me if I would like to learn to embroider and help her get ready for the baby. It was the first time she shared childbearing with me, and it made me feel all grown up.

Although Daddy raised another good crop that year, he didn't want to sharecrop again. Before the new baby was due, he had found a farm to rent six miles southeast of Claremore, near Tiawah, and we made plans to move.

Before we left Sequoyah, Daddy's youngest sister, Aunt Ida, filed for divorce. She and her two children stayed at our house for several weeks until her divorce was granted and she got custody of her children and permission to take them out of state. It was sad the night Uncle Clinton came and said good-bye. He cried when he left. Everyone cried, even Daddy. Still, I was too young to realize the seriousness of divorce. Mostly I was envious of my cousin Louise for getting to go live in California.

I rode with Daddy to Claremore to see them off. During the tearful good-bye, I heard Daddy say, "Now, don't you worry, Idie, we'll be out there with you soon—next year, I hope." I stood on the platform beside my dad and watched Ida and my cousins climb the steps into the train. She turned back and waved a final farewell and disappeared into the railcar. As the train jerked and moved slowly out of the station, we watched the windows for a glimpse of Aunt Ida and my cousins, but before we could see them, the train picked up speed, slid past us, and disappeared out of town.

Tiawah

THE MOVE TO TIAWAH had a different feel to it. It seemed as if we really would make it to California soon. Aunt Ada and Uncle Leonard were planning to return to California in the summer, and we would be the only ones of Daddy's family left in Oklahoma. Mama talked a lot about California, even though she was facing childbirth in a few days.

The farm belonged to the Eddy family. They were in California but planned to return and live out their lives in Oklahoma. We rented it for two hundred dollars a year. Daddy sold the pickup to help pay the rent. Then he applied for a government loan to buy more cows. We moved in early December 1945, two months before my thirteenth birthday.

Our new home was a good size and had a well near the back door. The only trees were in a long plum thicket along a small stream in the pasture. For heat, we burned coal. All winter, black soot seemed to cover everything, but the living room was warm.

Soon after we moved in, Daddy and Robert went to the livestock auction. With the loan Daddy was able to set us up with sixteen good milk cows and all the milking equipment we needed. Everyone who was old enough was in the milk barn morning and evening. A truck from the Claremore creamery stopped early in the day, and the driver picked up a ten-gallon can of milk. Every two weeks he delivered a check.

All those aluminum buckets and utensils had to be washed and sterilized. If the creamery received sour milk, they returned it. We didn't mind, because it meant homemade cottage cheese. Mama filled a large pan with clabbered milk and set it on the stove. As the milk warmed, the curds and whey separated. Tink and I placed a clean dish towel over the top of a milk bucket and secured it with clothespins. We dipped out the warm curds with a ladel and strained it with the cloth. After it drained into the bucket, we removed the clothespins and squeezed with all our might to remove any remaining whey. Mama emptied the curds into a large bowl, added butter, salt, and black pepper and a little cream she had skimmed from the top. I have never seen anything like Mama's homemade cottage cheese in a grocery store.

Even the whey wasn't wasted. We fed it to the hogs. They rushed to the fence, pushing and shoving, climbing over one another and rooting and fighting until the trough was empty.

Early on the morning of December 13, 1945, Mama woke me. It was still dark. She said, "Get up, honey, and be quiet so we don't wake the other kids." Daddy had built a fire, but the living room was still cold. I wrapped myself in a blanket and shivered by the stove, trying to get warm.

Mama said, "You'll have to stay home today and take care of the babies. Daddy's takin' me to the hospital in Claremore. He'll be back this evenin' and I'll be home in a few days with our new baby. Do you understand?"

"Yeah. Where's Daddy now?"

"He walked down to get Mr. Roden. He told Daddy to come day or night and he'd take us in his car. They're good neighbors."

A few minutes later, I heard Mr. Roden's big black sedan pull up in the driveway. Daddy came in and picked up the little bundle of baby things and helped Mama to the car. Before they left, he said, "Wake Robert and Sid in a few minutes. It's almost time to do the milkin'. Tink'll help 'em. You stay here with the babies and fix breakfast. I'll be back after while. Tell the other kids to go to school."

I stayed home with three-year-old Susie and June and Judy, who were five. About an hour after the other kids got home from school, Mr. Roden brought Daddy home.

"Mama has another baby girl," he told us. "She has pretty dark hair and blue eyes. Mama will be there a few more days before she brings her home. We named her Kathryn Ann after Grandma Bristol. What do you say we call her Kitty?"

The name stuck. She's always been Kitty.

In a few days an ambulance came and two men dressed in white carried Mama into the house on a stretcher. Daddy brought Kitty in. She was wrapped snugly in a pink blanket, asleep.

At dinner Mama said it felt so good to be home, but she was worrying about a young woman she had met at the hospital. She said, "I watched Molly walk them halls for three days. I wish she'd had that baby before I left."

"I'll ask about her," Daddy said. "Or I'll see if Mr. Roden will find out about her."

A few days later, Mr. Roden brought word that Molly and her baby had died. Her baby had been breach, and in the 1940s, they didn't perform cesarean sections after the onset of labor. Mama, with her big family, couldn't forget that young woman who died trying to have her first child.

🙟

The winter of eighth grade, I discovered basketball. I was tall for my age and Mr. Piguet, the coach, gave me a position as guard. I didn't daydream on the basketball court. Before long I was stealing the ball so fast I surprised myself, and I was having the time of my life.

Meanwhile, Robert spent a lot of time alone, sometimes just sitting on the merry-go-round. He claimed not to like sports, but I think he was homesick for Sequoyah. One day a bus pulled up from Sequoyah High School, and as the basketball players piled off, Robert ran to meet them, happier than I had seen him since we moved. They won both games. While I rooted for my new friends, Robert sat with the Sequoyah kids. He stood in the school yard waving to them as they pulled away that evening. On the way home, he said, "Man, I wish I could've got on that bus and went home with them guys."

Finally, he found a buddy named Bill. Both of them loved horses. That next summer they did farm work together and went to Saturday movies in Claremore. They were close friends as long as we lived at Tiawah.

⌇⌇

The girls from the high school team left their basketball shoes in the dressing room so we younger girls could borrow them during our practice. Many of us didn't own tennis shoes. We all scrambled through the tangled pile. Sometimes I came up with a pair that was too big, but I was happy to have any shoes, just so I could play.

Daddy wouldn't allow Tink and me to wear shorts, or even khakies. So I played my heart out in a little pink and white gingham dress with a gathered skirt. I knew Daddy's religion forbade girls to wear shorts, and seldom did he compromise, but I had a new love and nothing was going to keep me off the basketball court.

While Mama took care of Kitty that winter, Tink and I went into Claremore with Daddy on Saturdays to do the laundry. Mama gave us instructions over and over as if I'd never done it before and didn't know it all by heart. Daddy had sold our pickup, so we had to take the old horse-drawn wagon to town. Tink and I sat in the back, bundled up with our feet dangling. We were warmer there than we would have been in front, and besides, I was so embarrassed, I rode the full six miles hoping no one would see me coming to town in the back of a horse-drawn wagon.

When we were done and Daddy was finished shopping, he loaded the wet laundry into the wagon and we walked down the street to a tiny snack bar. Tink and I climbed onto bar stools and ate five-cent burgers while Daddy ate chili and crackers. Then we left for the long, cold ride home.

Once in a while he gave us each a quarter and waited while we shopped at Woolworth's five and dime store. The first time we went, I spent my quarter on my first bottle of Blue Waltz perfume, a popular "dimestore scent." The bottle was shaped like a heart, with a blue budlike cap, and I loved the fragrance.

One Saturday as we headed out of town toward Tiawah, a big black sedan pulled alongside us and stopped. It was the Gabbards. Mrs. Gabbard was Robert's and my Sunday school teacher. She asked if Tink and I would like to ride with them and get in out of the cold, saying Daddy could pick us up when he passed their house. Daddy said we could. Tink and I were reluctant, but we climbed into the car. I remember both of us looking through the back window at Daddy sitting all alone on the wagon seat in the cold as we rode out of sight.

The Gabbards were nice, though. Mrs. Gabbard brought chairs in from the dining room and sat with us by the fire and gave us hot chocolate. Her name was Willie and most people called her Sister Bill. She looked tall and matronly in her simple housedress, and she was warm and cheerful. She wore her light brown hair off her face, twisted pompadour style in front with a bun at the back of her neck. She asked us how we were doing in school and church, and then said she had heard me sing in the choir. She invited me to come with her to a singing convention in Collinsville in the summer, to represent the church. She said I could choose what I wanted to sing.

That conversation began a friendship that lasted the two years we lived in Tiawah and continued by mail for a long time after. I did go with her in the summer, and when she had parties, she asked me to help her plan them and get things ready.

On that day, though, Tink and I worried about Daddy out in the cold. We kept walking to the window and watching for him, until we saw him come into sight. We said good-bye and thanks and ran out the door. Then we jumped aboard with Daddy and rode past the school and around the hill to home.

࿐

One cold February morning, we woke to a beautiful blanket of snow. It was ankle deep. With Daddy leading the way, we waded out to the barn to milk the cows. Tink, Sid, and I carried scoops of grain from the storage room and dumped them into the cows' stalls while Robert and Daddy brought the animals in from the barnyard. In they came, single file, through the small door, rushing for their food. Baby switched her tail across her back, throwing snow all over me as I pulled a long slanting board to a vertical position and slipped a cord over the top, fastening her head in the stall. She kicked at the touch of my cold hands, but settled down as they warmed against her udders.

Our old gray cat positioned himself against the wall behind the cows. Robert waited until Daddy wasn't looking and shot a stream of milk across the barn into the cat's mouth. Sid snickered, then angled a cow's teat in the same direction until the stream ran out. The cat lapped as fast as he could. We all laughed, forgetting the cold, even Daddy, but not for long.

"That's enough," he said. "Put the milk in the bucket. That cat ain't gonna go hungry. There's plenty of mice around here for him."

That morning at breakfast we heard Daddy's usual complaint about how slow I milked. He said, "A cow will hold up her milk if you don't work fast."

Mama said, "Betty works at a slow steady pace. Don't matter if she weeds corn or sweeps the floor. She works slow, but she don't stop; she keeps movin'."

"I know, but Tink can strip a cow of every ounce of milk she's got. Betty can't."

I knew what he was leading up to. I liked going to the milk barn, but he said, "You're gonna have to stay at the house and cook breakfast for a while, and we'll see how it goes."

Robert said, "Sure gonna miss Mama's cookin'."

Everyone laughed, even me.

While we got ready for school, Daddy swept snow from the wagon and hitched up the team. Snow was falling lightly as the team stopped in front of the school. The only tracks visible were those cut through the snow by the wagon wheels as they wound around the hill behind us. At day's end Daddy was there to pick us up.

The Eddy place had two ponds. Livestock drank from the one in the barnyard and the other was in the pasture with the pigs. Both ponds froze in the winter. Daddy broke ice around the edges to let the animals drink. Teenagers from the church in Tiawah gathered at our house on Sunday afternoons to skate, and with our big family and all our friends, it was a party every week. None of us owned ice skates. We just ran to get up speed, jumped, and hit the ice, skidding as fast and far as our shoes would take us. If we could round up old shoes, we used them, but if not, we used our good shoes.

Robert's new cowboy boots didn't do so well on the ice. The first time he tried to slide, both feet went out from under him and he sprawled on the pond, covered with ice and snow. The girls laughed, his face turned red, and he stood around on the bank the rest of the afternoon. I told him to go get his old shoes on, but he wouldn't. He said, "I'd die if I did that again. I ain't gonna take no chances." He'd rather watch and laugh at us taking spills.

༄

At the end of basketball season we went into Claremore for one week to participate in the tournament. Our junior high teams, both boys and girls, played during the day, and we watched other teams compete. When it came our turn to play, we won every game, eliminating rival teams from the competition. By Friday, we were tied for first place with the girls from Verdigris. I was happy when one of the girls on their team joined the game wearing a dress. We all played a close, intense game right up to the end. With eight seconds to go, we were behind by one point. One of their guards fouled and Esther, our best forward, got two free shots. She made them both, putting us one point in the lead. It was their ball. I stole it and threw it across the center line to Lee, who dribbled in closer to the basket and passed it to Esther for a chance to score. It went out of bounds and the other team took the ball. I don't remember how it happened, only that one of their girls sank the ball through the hoop and I heard the loud, blaring sound of the buzzer. My stomach sank as the Verdigris team leaped into the air.

We took home the sportsmanship trophy, but there were tears in the dressing room and all the way home. Mr. Piguet tried to console us by saying how proud of us he was, but it was no use. Verdigris took home the trophy we wanted, the trophy we lost by one lousy point.

Our first year at Tiawah school drew to a close, and with it came my eighth-grade graduation. There were five boys and three girls—Esther, Doris, and I. Four seniors graduated from high school.

Before the big day, Esther and Doris brought their graduation dresses to school and asked me if I would like to get one like theirs. They were two-piece, navy blue, taffeta sailor dresses with wide collars squared off from shoulder to shoulder in the back. They were trimmed with three narrow white stripes and a white silky tie that lay under the collar and tied just below the V in front. I could see myself in that dress, and I hurried home to tell Mama, "They bought them at Penney's for $2.98."

I had never had a store-bought dress before, since Mama was such a good seamstress. She said she couldn't promise; we would have to ask Daddy. He said I could buy it, that he wanted me to dress like the other girls. When I tried it on, I just knew I'd outshine everyone at graduation, including the high school seniors.

Friday night, I walked to school with Robert and Tink. Once inside, we saw Alma Ott sitting at the piano in her cap and gown. To the tune of "Pomp and Circumstance," I marched down the aisle in my store-bought dress with Esther, Doris, and the five eighth-grade boys. I guess we must have looked like sailors straight off a boat to the audience, with the war still fresh in their minds, because everyone gasped when they saw us. Then all of us graduating students sat on the stage for the ceremony.

I hadn't thought of how it would feel to walk across the stage alone when my name was called. At that moment, I wanted to slip behind the curtain out of sight, but I was stuck. Taking my turn on stage was part of the deal.

When I got back to my seat, I realized that when I came back next year, I would be a high school freshman.

Our first summer on the Eddy place, Daddy bought another Model A pickup. It was just like the little red one we had had, except it was black. Every Sunday he drove us to the Assembly of God Church in Claremore. Daddy had taken Tink and me there a few times earlier to hear Brother Haymaker talk of God's love and grace. I remember it was an old, small building.

When we went back, though, we discovered a brand-new structure. The main auditorium could seat three hundred people. Down each side, partitions separated three Sunday school classrooms. Burgundy velvet curtains, drawn across the front of each partition, could be pulled back to seat more people if needed.

June, Judy, and Sid went with us on Sunday mornings. If Daddy had enough gas for another trip, he took Tink and me again on Sunday evenings. Those evenings were a treat for us because he almost always stopped at the little store in Tiawah on the way home and bought us each a Pepsi-Cola.

Mention of the church in Claremore wouldn't be complete without the Dixon sisters. They were attractive young women, about five feet, seven inches tall. All three had shoulder-length hair worn in the latest styles of the forties. One was blond, one brunette, and the third had beautiful auburn hair. They sang three-part harmony before the Sunday evening sermon and to me, the Dixon sisters just *were* the church in Claremore. That was about the time I began singing harmony with Tink. Her low soft voice blended with my high one, and I would sing all day if I could get her to sing with me. When Mama and Daddy made a trip to town, we cleaned house while two-part harmony wafted through every window and door.

Late one evening, as I was gathering clothes from the line, I noticed a tall stranger walking down the hill past the Roden house. He was carrying an old brown cardboard suitcase and looking at our house. I ran to Mama and said, "Do you know that man? I think he's comin' here."

She pushed the kitchen curtain aside. "That's Ivan. Addie said he might be comin' to see his brother. Maybe he'll talk to Daddy about California. Run out to the barn and tell Daddy he's here."

Daddy was cleaning out the cow stalls. I said, "Daddy, Uncle Ivan's here." He stepped outside, stood his shovel against the barn door, and started toward the house. The two men embraced and cried. They were kin by marriage, but both said they felt like brothers.

I followed them to the house, anxious to hear them talk about California.

While they washed up, Tink and I put supper on the table. Mama put Ivan on her chair at the end and joined us children on one of the two benches that sat along both sides of the table.

"Elsie, did you make these benches?" Uncle Ivan asked.

Before she could answer, Daddy said, "Ain't them the finest benches you ever seen? Elsie's always been handy like that. She makes all the girls' clothes. Cuts her patterns outta newspapers. And me and the boys never go to the barber shop." He laughed. "You know I didn't make them benches, don't you. I can't drive a straight nail." We all laughed.

Uncle Ivan said, "I bet he can still plow a straight row with a team of horses, though, can't he, Elsie?"

Mama smiled and nodded her head.

Uncle Ivan went on. "I guess you know I got strict orders from Addie to bring you all back with me, or at least talk as hard as I can to get you to start makin' plans. You wouldn't be sorry."

I searched Daddy's face. He dropped his head and stared at a spot on the table, his mind far away for a few seconds. Then he said to Uncle Ivan, "You've got along pretty good out there, ain't you?"

Uncle Ivan had just warmed up. He talked about the San Joaquin Valley, the cotton fields, the irrigation. How there were lots of jobs, right through the long picking time, and how Daddy could drive a tractor. Daddy listened hard, and Mama pulled herself closer to the table. She said, "You could do that, Daddy. And I could pick cotton. Me and the kids could help."

Robert said, "I could work in the fields, too."

I could hardly sit still. I cried, "Me too! I could work too!"

"Wait a minute here," Daddy said. "I ain't said for sure we're goin'."

But Mama wouldn't let it go. She asked how much cotton Aunt Addie could pick, and he said sometimes five hundred pounds in a day. Mama gasped at that. She said, "My goodness, two hundred would be a good day's work for me."

Daddy laughed and said that would be a good day's work for him, too. He was troubled about the trip, though. He said, "You know, Ivan, I ain't never drove any further than from here into Claremore. How can I take off across country, almost two thousand miles, with a wife and eight kids?"

"But Bill, Route 66 runs right through Claremore. All you gotta do is head west and follow the 66 signs all the way across the California border to Barstow."

"We're doing good here," Daddy said. "Maybe next year I can pay off the government loan and buy a pickup with cash left over. I mean it, Ivan, I'd like to leave these cold winters behind."

"Maybe next year," again. I'd heard it many times and so had Mama. Still, when Uncle Ivan said good-bye and boarded the train, he left us with higher hopes than ever before.

⌁

Then Aunt Ada's family returned to California. Her oldest son, who had been staying with Aunt Addie and working in the fields for more than a year, was able to send enough money for the whole family to take the train out. They had been living on Grandpa Gore's place during that time. I went with Daddy to pick them up and take them to the depot, and that was the last time I saw that big yellow house.

By then I was accustomed to watching trains come and go, but when once again I hugged my cousins as Daddy and Aunt Ada said their good-byes, I cried. Even though the war was over, there were still young men in uniforms on the train, some of them probably on their way home. They waved and reached out to us as the train pulled away, but I had my eyes on Aunt Ada and her family.

After they left, a sadness fell over me that lasted all summer. Mama talked about Aunt Addie's linoleum floors and electric lights and washing machine. When I asked, "Do you think we'll move next year?" she said she was afraid to get her hopes too high and that Daddy's memories of his childhood still affected his thoughts about a long trip. Mama said, "I feel sorry for him. He says things like, 'I wish we was already there' and 'It's a long hard trip. What if the pickup breaks down? What if one of the kids gets sick?' His parents lost three kids on them long trips between Missouri and Oklahoma, and they buried 'em and moved on. He's just plain scared."

Mama said she tried to tell him things were different, that Route 66 was a safe highway and if we had trouble, we could get help. And that there was lots of work in the farming country. He could drive a tractor. "Look at him out there in the field," she said. "You see how hard he fights to keep the plow in the ground? It takes a strong man to do that, and he comes in all tired out. I wish he didn't have to work so hard."

I looked in the direction of the field. I was thirteen, and I had grown up watching my daddy plow with a team of horses. All that time, it had never occurred to me how much strength it took to turn the soil.

I can still see him with both hands on the plow, pressing with all his might to keep the blade in the ground, heaving the handles from one side and then the other to keep the rows straight. He sang everything from "Rock of Ages" to "Let the Midnight Special Shine Its Light on Me" as Tink and I walked along behind him in the freshly plowed earth.

Mama never talked about all the work she did. By the end of summer, she would have filled dozens of fruit jars from the cellar beneath the kitchen with peaches, plums, green beans, tomatoes, blackberries, sauerkraut, and pickles. Tink and I carried the jars upstairs and helped Mama wash them in a washtub to get ready for canning. She worked hard to keep us fed through the winter months.

❧

On November 4, Claremore celebrated Will Rogers's birthday with a rodeo and parade. Robert rode his new saddle horse into town, and Daddy took the rest of us, except Mama and Kitty, who was nearing her first birthday. A large crowd lined the main street.

Daddy kept us together and found a spot where we could sit on the curb with a good view of the parade.

It was my first time to see a marching band. There were sixteen bands in the parade that day, some from as far away as Arkansas and Kansas. Majorettes in high-top boots and short uniforms pranced and twirled batons, marching in front of the musicians, keeping perfect time with the music. The bands were all decked out in colorful uniforms—blue and gold, burgundy and gold, white and gold. I had never seen such a display of colors.

As we were leaving, Daddy led us down the street to the J.C. Penney store and surprised me. He said, "Do you think you can find a pair of shoes for basketball here?"

I picked out a pair of high tops and he laid a couple of one-dollar bills on the counter. I walked out clutching a box of shoes to my chest, my head held high. I was thrilled down to my toes, ready for basketball to start.

That year, the boys team included three American GIs who had returned home and enrolled to get their high school diplomas. The Hodges boy had been a navy man. Leon and Alan Forbes had served in the army. All three were tall, experienced players. They joined Robert's friend Bill, who had become a good athlete, and, with the other players, won almost every game.

They made the finals in the Claremore tournament and my excitement for them was as high as it had been for my own team the year before. The morning of the final game, a white light through my window awoke me. Outside was a blanket of blinding snow.

After chores, Mama and Daddy debated keeping us home from school. When I protested, saying that it was the boys team playoffs and everyone was going into town on the bus, Daddy relented and took me to school in the wagon. The pickup was under several inches of snow.

When we came in sight of the school, my eyes searched for the big yellow bus. At first I thought maybe it was parked where I couldn't see it. I jumped out of the wagon and ran. The gym was empty. Finally I saw one of the cafeteria cooks. She said the bus had waited for me for a while, but they gave me up, because of the snow. They were gone.

"I tried so hard to get here," I said, almost crying.

"Why don't you help me?" she said. She was peeling potatoes. So I helped her with the stew. In the afternoon I went to the school library and read Nancy Drew's *The Hidden Staircase*.

When at last the bus pulled in, the coach stepped off with a big gold trophy. It was mounted on a wooden base with a gold plaque inscribed for the Tiawah High School boys basketball team, champions for the school year 1946–47. The girls team, which I had been a part of, received the sportsmanship trophy once again.

✌

Before I knew it, it was summer again, and Mama was canning fruit. I asked why we were canning so much if we might be moving to California. She said, "Honey, you know Daddy. He ain't said for sure we're goin'." Then she sent me off with Sid and the little girls to the plum thicket for more plums. Sid played with the cows, climbing on their backs and riding until they bucked him to the ground. Baby ran through the plum thicket and dragged him off. He laughed and cried at the same time while we pulled him from a tangled mess among the tree limbs.

Aunt Ada's son, who was almost seventeen, came for a visit in a 1937 Oldsmobile coupe and two of Aunt Addie's teenagers were with him. That same week, two of Mama's nephews arrived. One of them, T.C., was sixteen, and we hadn't seen him since he was eleven. He had grown to be almost seven feet tall. Our cousin James was with him. He took the car to visit other relations for a few days and left T.C. with us.

One day Robert asked if he could take our cousins in the pickup to visit the Will Rogers Memorial in Claremore. Daddy said no because Robert didn't have his driver's license. But Robert did have a permit, and T.C. had a license, so Robert asked if he could drive partway.

Daddy was quiet for a minute and then said, "All right. You can drive to the highway. But when you get to the main road, stop and let one of the older boys drive into town." Robert agreed.

The boys crowded into the cab. Sid rode in the back with us girls.

We drove past the school and through the little town of Tiawah. Just before the main road, we had to cross the railroad tracks. There were no lights, no bells, and no arms to drop down and stop traffic. The boys failed to see a locomotive bearing down on the crossing. Robert hit his brake and slowed up to cross over. The pickup stalled on the tracks.

The engineer tugged at the whistle as it screamed at us to get out of the way, but there was no time. We jumped out of the back. T.C. and the others, packed in like sardines, climbed out the passenger side, but Robert struggled to get his door open. The latch was broken and Daddy had rigged it with baling wire to keep it shut.

I ran to help him. He pushed and kicked at the door and I wrestled with the wire. Suddenly T.C.'s big frame reached in and dragged Robert out the other side, and we ran clear of the tracks.

People standing outside the store had turned their backs to keep from seeing us killed.

The train hit the pickup broadside, shoved it several yards down the tracks, and tore it to pieces. Amid the noise and confusion, I started toward the mangled piece of wreckage. Someone grabbed my arm and pulled me back. A loud screeching sound filled the air as heavy iron wheels scraped the tracks. I couldn't hear what T.C. was saying to me. The noisy freight cars clanged against one another all the way down the line. When I finally was able to understand my cousin, I realized he thought I had been hit. I thought he and Robert had been caught in the path of the train.

I ran to Robert, who sat sobbing in the gravel by the road, wiping tears on his shirt sleeve.

When we got home, Mama and Daddy gave thanks that none of us were hurt or killed. Daddy said, "A pickup can be replaced. The life of one of my kids is too precious to give up."

A couple of weeks later a man from the railroad came to our house and questioned Robert and me. He said he had to make a report. Daddy kept saying, "You can't replace a life. Me and Mama's so thankful," repeating all the things he had said the day we came home. For weeks he waited anxiously, hoping the railroad might replace his truck, but he never heard a word from them.

After that, he rode into town with Mr. Roden. One Saturday, Mama said, "I'm going with Daddy to buy groceries. I want to pick out a flour sack with them little pink flowers so I can make Susie a dress. Daddy might bring home the wrong print."

I stayed home to clean the kitchen while Tink took the babies out to play. I was putting dishes away when I saw an envelope stashed behind a stack of plates. I saw that it was from Grandma Bristol. It had been opened, so I took it out to read.

"The last thing you and Bill need is another baby," Grandma had written. "If you're due in late September, how in the world are you gonna be able to make a long trip this fall? Every time you have a baby, I keep hoping it'll be the last. But this time, well, I don't know what to say. You just ain't got no need for another baby!"

Grandma went on to say that she and Grandpa were planning to come see us in the fall. Grandpa wanted to see his brothers, and then they were hoping to help us get ready to move.

By the time I finished the letter, tears were rolling down my face. I wiped them with the back of my hand. Hurt was mixed with anger.

"I'm tired of babies," I thought. "We got enough babies!" I sat on a bench, laid my face on the table, and cried.

When Mama and Daddy got back, Daddy dug potatoes. I spent most of the afternoon working off part of my disappointment by picking up potatoes. We carried buckets of them into a small room in the corner the milk barn and spread them on the wooden floor. Some had been cut in half by the plow. Those we took to the house to be used first. For supper we had new potatoes and creamed peas. I never mentioned the letter to anyone.

Holy Water

ONE EVENING IN SEPTEMBER, I filled the wash pan with warm water and lined the babies up. One by one, the four of them took their place on a little wooden chair and dangled their feet in the water. I was helping them get ready for bed when I heard Daddy talking to Mama about California. He said in order to keep the family together, it seemed like the time had come for us to leave.

"Robert and Betty's growin' up. Before long they'll be gettin' married, and we could never go off and leave one of the kids. You reckon by the first of November you'll be able to make a trip?"

"Oh sure, Daddy," Mama said. "That'd give me five or six weeks. I'll be all right!"

"The rent's paid 'til January, but I'd like to cross the mountains before the weather gets bad, and I hope we can make it to California in time to pick some cotton before the season ends."

I couldn't believe what I was hearing. I didn't say a word. Somehow I knew that from that moment on, it was understood: we were leaving as soon as our cotton was picked and hauled into the gin.

On September 25 our brother Jimmy was born, and Mama spent three days in the hospital in Claremore.

I was in the middle of a baseball game. Someone hit a fly ball and I ran under it. Just before it hit my glove, I jerked my hands back and stepped from under the ball. It hit the ground and everyone laughed. Baseball was not my game.

Someone yelled, "There goes an ambulance."

Cal Lucas said, "Ain't you heard? Mrs. Grant had another baby. Just what they need, another kid." I felt like hitting him with the bat.

I ran all the way home, with my siblings at my heels. As we raced through the door, Mama shushed us and said, "Slow up, I just cleaned him and got him to sleep."

Jimmy was on a pillow wearing only a diaper. He wasn't skinny like most newborns. He was short and husky, with broad shoulders and plump arms and legs, and lots of dark hair. My heart melted.

Mama said, "Peel some potatoes for supper. He'll wake up soon enough." When I was finally allowed to hold him, I knew he was one of us, as if he had always been around.

☙

Friends came after school every day to help us pick cotton. Daddy put out an old set of scales that dangled from a three-legged wooden stand. A piece of rope was tied to a metal hook at the bottom of the scales. He wrapped the rope around the middle of a sack of cotton, let the sack dangle below the scales, and took off a pound or sometimes two for the sack. He paid us two cents a pound.

☙

Tink and I had been talking about being baptized. One warm September evening, the church at Tiawah took a group of new converts to the river after church services and Brother Newman asked if we would like to be baptized too. Tink and I knew Daddy didn't agree with that church's method of baptizing, so we took off around the hill with Robert. We were probably in bed and asleep before the rest of the congregation got home.

At breakfast the next day, we told Mama and Daddy about the Tiawah baptisms, and Daddy said, "It ain't right he would baptize you girls knowin' I wouldn't like it." Then he asked us if we wanted to be baptized.

We looked and each other, smiled, and nodded our heads. All our friends were being baptized, even our cousin Louise, out in California. So Daddy said he would talk to his friend Brother Ott about baptizing us the following Sunday, before we left for California.

A feeling of peace swept over me. Tink looked excited as she smiled at me. We didn't know Brother Ott well, but we had been to his services in the Rucker schoolhouse a few times. Mostly older people went there, and we liked being with our friends in Tiawah, but for us to be baptized by Daddy's friend seemed like the perfect solution.

Grandma and Grandpa Bristol were visiting relatives in Wagoner. They had had train tickets for their return to California in a few days. Mama wrote them about our plans to be baptized. At noon on Sunday, they arrived in Uncle Ed and Aunt Jane's Ford sedan, just in time for dinner.

While Uncle Ed helped Grandpa unload suitcases, Aunt Jane went to Daddy as he stood in the middle of the yard with his hands tucked inside the bib of his overalls. Quietly, she asked him if he thought the preacher would baptize her, too. Daddy assured her he would see that she was among the ones immersed in Jones's pond that afternoon.

We sat down to Mama's fried chicken dinner and Grandpa said grace. Uncle Ed declared the meal fit for a king. Then the conversation shifted to talk of the California journey. Finally Daddy told Tink and me to clean up the kitchen and get ready to leave for church. The baptism would be at two o'clock. He then went out to the barn with the other men.

Once the men were gone, Grandma opened her suitcase and took out an old faded dress for Aunt Jane to wear. She told Mama she had hidden it from Uncle Ed because he didn't approve of Jane's being baptized. Mama was astonished that Aunt Jane was planning to go ahead without telling Uncle Ed, and that Daddy didn't know about the deception.

Aunt Jane began rocking her body, holding her hands over her mouth, nearly wailing as she said, "He wouldn't have heared to it! I'm sixty-four years old, and I want to be baptized before I die!"

Mama put her arms around Jane. "Honey, you got a right to be baptized. But Ed not knowin'? You know how Bill is. He'll have a fit."

Tink and I changed into old clothes. I had never been so nervous, thinking about being dunked in the waters of baptism, nor so excited.

The men were in the barnyard for a long time. When they walked back into the yard, Tink and I dashed to the car. Grandma walked out with Jane half-hidden behind her. At the top of the porch steps, Aunt Jane hesitated. She stood there in her faded, wrinkled old dress, her head down, wondering if it was safe to go down into the yard.

Uncle Ed stood tall and straight, with his hands on his hips. He cocked his head to one side and aimed his eyes straight at her until she looked up. She had to face him. Daddy looked stunned.

Grandma went over to Grandpa. There was a moment of terrible waiting, and then Uncle Ed broke the silence. Maybe he surveyed the family and realized he was outnumbered. "Ah hell, woman," he blurted, "get in the car."

Daddy didn't allow swearing around his family, but this time he didn't say a word. He climbed into the car and waved at Mama, who was watching from inside the screen door.

There were four of us at Rucker School to be baptized. A teenage boy had joined our family. Brother Ott led us to Jones's pond. On the bank, about fifteen people stood and sang, "Shall We Gather at the River." Then Brother Ott read from the Book of Mark, where Jesus is baptized by John in the muddy river of Jordan. After a few words of his own, he waded into the water up to his waist.

A few yards downstream, a couple of cows waded out into a shallow spot to drink. Farther down, another cow was drinking from the bank. All of them lifted their heads and watched curiously.

Brother Ott motioned us into the water. He took Aunt Jane by the hand and helped her over beside him. He lifted her arms and crossed them over her chest. He asked her if she believed in the Father, Son, and Holy Ghost, and if she claimed Jesus as her personal savior. With tears streaming down her face, she answered, "Yes, I do."

Placing his left hand on the back of her head and holding her nose and mouth with his right hand, Brother Ott said, "Jane, I baptize you in the name of the Father, and of the Son, and of the Holy Ghost." Then he tipped her backward into the water, immersing her whole body into the muddy pond.

She emerged, gasping for air, spitting water. She coughed a few times as Brother led her to the water's edge. Grandma wrapped her dripping body in a dry blanket that Mama had sent.

One by one, Brother Ott dunked the three of us teenagers in the same manner. I was greatly relieved when it was over.

Uncle Ed helped a shivering Aunt Jane into the car. Turning to Brother Ott, he reached out his hand and said, "Thank you very much, Reverend. Fine baptizin'."

As we drove away I thought how Mama had forbidden us to go swimming during those years of polio epidemic. I wondered if she understood what we had just done in a pond. I savored the sacredness of it, and I never said a word about the immersion to worry Mama.

I have witnessed many baptisms over the years, done in many different ways. None compares to that Sunday afternoon when we shared our baptismal waters with Mr. Jones's cows. Or was it the other way around? On our baptismal certificate, Brother Ott kindly referred to our baptistry as "Jones Tank." Tink and I were able to leave for our new life as baptized travelers.

Sale Day

ON SATURDAY WE PICKED our last rows of cotton, loaded the wagon, and parked it until we could take it to the gin on Monday. On Sunday, Daddy said, "Since we're leaving, we can surely have a good dinner today. Robert, you and Sid help me catch a couple chickens." Mama met Daddy and the boys at the back door with a spring in her step, and went about her chores singing, "I have blessed peace with my Lord so near, leaning on the everlasting arms."

She boiled a bucket of water and I helped her carry it to the edge of the porch. We dipped the dead chickens into the water to scald their feathers. Then we plucked the feathers until the carcasses were clean. Back in the kitchen, Mama cut the chickens into pieces and placed them in flour on a platter. I rolled each one to coat it before putting it in a pan of hot grease to cook.

While we were working, Mama said, "Betty, I want you to stay home from school tomorrow. Daddy's goin' to town, and you can take Susie with you and do the laundry. We need to get things ready for our trip."

"We're really gonna leave this time, ain't we, Mama?"

"I'm sure we are," she said, "but I ain't gonna let myself think about it too much."

Susie and I rode in with Daddy on our last load of cotton. I have a vivid memory of the two of us perched atop the white load on two pillowcases filled with dirty laundry. It was a rare opportunity for five-year-old Susie, and years later I would look back and see I was lucky to be with Daddy that day, too.

Susie scooted close to me as the team pulled onto the gravel road toward Tiawah. Daddy looked back at us and smiled as we laughed and kept time with the sway of the wagon bouncing along in the gravel.

When we passed the school, we saw June and Judy playing on the merry-go-round, and Susie cried, "I want to go to school at Tiawah next year!"

I hugged her close. "But we're goin' to California. You'll start school there."

"I don't wanna go anywhere but Tiawah."

I told her how we'd be going on a long trip and she wanted to know if we were traveling in the wagon. I laughed and then saw Daddy laughing, but I knew he couldn't hear us above the sound of the horses hooves and the noise of the wagon. I went on, telling her Daddy was getting a pickup, and that we would be living near our cousins.

"Don't you remember Floyd?"

Floyd had shown her and Kitty a lot of special attention when he visited a few months earlier. She seemed to brighten when I mentioned him.

"And we'll see the ocean with the big rock stickin' out of the water."

"Oh yeah, the one in the picture."

I went on to remind her of things Aunt Addie had written about, and she was all smiles when we drove onto the main road leading into Claremore. With all my talk, it suddenly hit me that it was real. We were leaving in a week. Our plans had always been in the future, even as it came closer. I had been busy picking cotton, going to school, and caring for the babies. Now, sitting next to Susie on what

I knew was our last load of cotton, my spirits lifted as if I were floating in midair. I was struck with the realization that the hopes and dreams Mama had shared with me my entire childhood were about to become reality.

When it was dark, Daddy walked the floor and then went outside to pace in the yard. He made a trip to the barn and stayed a long time. Mama stepped out onto the porch and called to him, "Bill! Daddy! Please come in the house. Please try to get some rest."

His answer penetrated the darkness. "In a minute, Mama. I'm just checking on my livestock."

I asked Mama, "Can he still back out?"

"No, baby, I don't think so. He went to a lot of trouble settin' up the sale. I don't think he'll call it off now. Daddy wants to go, but he's scared. Don't say nothin'. Just go on to bed. He'll be all right in the morning. Things always look better in the light of day."

I couldn't sleep, worrying about Daddy. Finally he came into the house. He sat in the rocking chair and cried like a little child.

Mama was on the edge of the bed, feeding Jimmy a bottle. I watched through my bedroom door as she leaned toward Daddy, with tears in her eyes. "I don't know what to say, Daddy. What do you want me to do?"

"You can't do nothin', Mama, it's too late."

"Too late for what? Backin' out?"

"It breaks my heart to think about sellin' my cows and just drivin' away, but I sent out sale bills. I hired an auctioneer. The sale's set, that's that."

"But Daddy, we've talked about this trip for years. If we don't go now, we never will. We ain't got no family here. All our folks moved off and left us. Like you said, we gotta go while the family's still together. And we're gettin' outta here before the snow starts to fall. We're leavin' these cold winters behind."

"All I know right now is this seems like the most foolish thing I ever done. If I could back out, I'd do it. I'd call it off." He shook his head. "But it's too late."

Mama said, "You need to get some sleep. We're gonna be so busy, you won't have time to think. Next thing you know, we'll be on the road."

Daddy got up from his chair and took Jimmy in his arms. He stood in front of Mama looking down at him and said, "I can't believe we had another boy."

I drifted into a peaceful sleep, knowing we were California-bound.

᠀

Sale Day began like any other day, with milking chores. After breakfast, Tink and I were cleaning up the kitchen when the auctioneer drove his pickup into the yard. He and Daddy headed for the barn, and Robert sailed out the back door and followed. His friend, Bill, ran past the house, and I heard Robert say, "I knew you'd make it," and both of them laughed.

Soon there were other pickups and cars, pulling trailers. They lined the driveway and parked on the edge of the road. In a while, the auctioneer said, "Gather round, folks. We start in the barnyard." I could hear the loud repetition of auctioneer language. And then: "Sold to the man in the straw hat" or "the gentleman in the blue shirt, the overalls," and so on.

I walked around the smokehouse and out to the clothesline, trying to find a better view. I saw two men trying to load our favorite pet cow, Baby, into a trailer. She backed up and fought them. One of the men hit her with a leather strap and she lunged forward into the trailer. She struggled as the men fastened the tailgate. We had raised Baby from a calf and she had never known anyone but us. When they drove her past me, she raised her head as high as she could, and, turning toward me, she opened her mouth wide and bellowed. The pickup turned onto the road and drove away with Baby still looking back at the house and bawling.

By then it was midmorning and women from the church had arrived to make hamburgers. They brought a washtub filled with Pepsi and Nehi pop and set it on the back porch, covering the bottles with chunks of ice. A little later, I went down into the cellar and carried up the jars of brightly colored fruit and vegetables that Mama had canned. It seemed as if I had just put it all there. My friends Wanda and Lola showed up and helped me while we talked and laughed, mostly about boys.

Almost everything sold: cows and horses, pigs and chickens, farming tools, even the potatoes on the floor in the barn. Then the sale moved to the back porch. There were a few pieces of furniture worth selling, and they went on the auction block. Mama kept her Singer sewing machine and the two benches she had made. Through it all, she stood on the porch and watched the crowd. When the auctioneer held up a jar of peaches and said, "Look at that, folks. How'd you like to have a bowl of these settin' in front of you? Or maybe a nice peach cobbler?" a sad look came over Mama's face. She turned her back and went inside, where she stayed for the rest of the auction. Later she said, "I just couldn't watch them sell my pretty canned stuff."

Just as the sale ended, Grandma and Grandpa arrived with Uncle Ed and Aunt Jane. True to her word, Grandma had come to help Mama get ready for the trip.

After the crowd left, Daddy said, "Mr. Dyer offered me his Ford pickup for a fair price. I think we can make a nice trip in it. I'm goin' over to talk to him now." A while later, he drove up to the back door. Mama, Grandma, and Grandpa all gathered around to inspect the pickup.

"A fine truck, Bill," Grandpa roared in his usual loud voice. "You'll make a comfortable trip in this."

The next morning while we were at school, Daddy and Robert went into Claremore and paid off the government loan with the money from the auction. Daddy had a little less than two thousand dollars left to put in his pocket after that.

We ended our last day of school saying good-bye. Herbie, who was slower than the rest of us, had sat across from me in English class and liked to follow me around during lunch hour. On field trips, he hurried to the bus so he could save me a seat. I enjoyed him, he made me laugh, but I hadn't thought what our leaving would mean to him. I said good-bye to my other friends, and Herbie followed me right to the pickup.

Robert had come to drive us home. He walked out on the school grounds and said good-bye to friends. I got in the pickup and there was Herbie, looking at me, saying how much he was going to miss me. I said I would miss him, too, but no amount of words would ease the pain on his face. When Robert and the other kids got there and I closed my door, Herbie was hanging onto the handle. He leaned inside, saying again, "Gee, I'm gonna miss you guys." Finally Robert turned the key in the ignition and put the pickup in gear. He drove slowly, and Herbie followed alongside with his hand on the door for a few yards before he finally gave up and we drove off the school grounds.

৵

Grandma and Grandpa were leaving by train the next day, but that evening Grandma was determined to help Daddy arrange a comfortable place in the back of the truck for us kids to ride. The pickup bed had high wooden sideboards that would act as windbreakers. Daddy had rigged up a wooden roof, and he planned to rope a mattress on top to keep out the cold. Then he would set Mama's benches in the bed, one on each side, so we'd have a place to sit.

Grandma looked in and said, "Now, Bill, you make it comfortable for the kids to ride."

"Granny," he said, "how many times do I have to tell you these ain't your kids. Go back in the house and mind your own business."

Grandpa, who was almost totally deaf and couldn't hear what had been said, was watching from the back door. He opened the door for Grandma as she came up the steps. Inside, Grandma told Mama she should get out there and help, but Mama said, "Mommie, you oughta know Bill by now. It ain't gonna do no good to interfere. Besides," she said, "these kids are gonna have the time of their lives. Don't you know that?"

The next day, just before noon, Daddy took Grandma and Grandpa to town and saw them off on the train. That evening, Robert helped him secure things in the truck. Mama came out with a little wooden chair that had belonged to Aunt Sally when she was a baby. Grandma had given it to Mama and it had been passed down, one by one, to each of us kids. The sewing machine, the benches, and the little wooden chair were going to California with us.

When the truck was arranged and packed, we all went to bed, anxious to set out on our journey toward a home we knew nothing about. I lay awake on a folded quilt on the floor of my bedroom, too excited to sleep. My life would never be the same.

Route 66

MAMA WOKE ME to help her get the kids loaded. Daddy wanted to leave before first light. Mama said we could all go back to sleep in the truck. I looked through my bedroom door into the dimly lit living room. A tiny figure lay sleeping on a pillow. Our brother Jimmy was five weeks old.

Tink and I woke Susie, who was five, and June and Judy, who were seven. They were wearing flower-sack dresses, wrinkled but clean. We still called the three of them "the babies", and they did look so little at that early hour. Each cradled a rag doll she had gotten for Christmas. The girls wanted to take them, but Mama said no, because Daddy said we couldn't take extra stuff. They rubbed their sleepy eyes and dragged their feet as we led them outside and helped them into the truck. Daddy and Robert had placed a feather mattress on the pickup bed. The babies crawled to the back, grabbed a pillow each, and rolled up in quilts.

Mama and I went back to the house to check things out. There were a few empty fruit jars. The rickety table we had used as an ironing board was covered with clothes we had outgrown or worn out. Two old irons and three kerosene lamps were being left behind. The lamp in the living room was an amber-colored Aladdin with a long round wick that soaked up more kerosene than the others and burned more brightly.

In the room Tink and I had shared, there was a heap in the corner: a few old clothes, schoolbooks, and hair rollers made of long

strips of tin from a coffee can, wrapped in paper. I saw a faded ban-
danna and a couple of small blue bottles partly full of Blue Waltz
perfume.

Mama said, "I'd like to take that pretty Aladdin lamp. Mommie
give it to me. But we won't need it where we're goin.' And it'd probably just get broke anyway."

Outside, Robert stood by the door of the cab with two-year-old
Kitty in his arms. Mama climbed in and Daddy handed her the sleeping baby. As Robert got into the cab, I climbed over the tailgate of
the truck and joined my siblings. Mama looked through the back
window to see that we were safe and comfortable.

As Daddy pulled away, we heard a loud crunch. The pickup had
caught the edge of the porch and pulled a board loose. My heart
sank. Knowing Daddy, we might be there a half-day while he fixed
it. But he picked it up and laid it on the porch. Then he circled the
smokehouse and drove down the long driveway and onto the gravel
road. At that early hour, a dim light shone through the Rodens'
kitchen window.

We heard Mr. Roden say, "I was hoping you'd stop."

"I seen your light," Daddy said. "I told Mama I'd like to see you
this mornin', but I wasn't aimin' to wake you."

Mrs. Roden came out to say good-bye too. She said she'd miss us,
especially us kids going back and forth to school every day.

I could tell by Daddy's voice that the good-byes were tearful. As
we backed out of the driveway, the Rodens called out, "Write to us!"

The babies were asleep as we drove through Tiawah. I found
myself shedding tears when we passed the school, and I remembered
all the good times I had had there. Moments later we turned west on
Route 66, leaving Claremore behind. The Mother Road would take
us all the way to the check-in station in Barstow, California.

༄

I opened my eyes again as daylight poured through the back of the pickup. Daddy stopped at a service station with a small grocery store and bought donuts, milk, and a thermos of coffee. He stepped to the back of the pickup and said, "How's my babies?" They all three smiled and reached for a donut. "That's what I wanted to see," he said. By noon we were in Oklahoma City. Driving through the sprawling metropolis, we must have been a familiar sight—another farm family, with our mattress on top of the truck. Mama kept motioning through the window at the scenery, as if she wanted to be sure we wouldn't miss anything. At the far edge of the city, Daddy stopped again and bought food and filled up with gas. A few miles out of town, he pulled off the highway and parked near a big shade tree.

Mama handed Jimmy to me, wrapped in a soft flannel blanket she had made. I talked to him and tried to get him to laugh, but he kicked and squirmed. Tink took him from me and laid him across her shoulder. He lifted his head and looked around as if to say, what a strange place this is.

The midday sun was warm. Mama spread a denim quilt on the ground underneath the tree. She said, "This old quilt is the handiest thing. The dead grass don't stick to it. Just pick it up and shake it right off." She had made it from strips of old overalls.

Daddy opened Pepsis and handed them around. There was bologna, a loaf of bread, and cupcakes. A can of Spam, with its little metal key on the side, was something new. We watched Daddy pull the key and twist, splitting the can so the Spam fell out onto the plate in a block ready to be sliced. Ask any of my brothers and sisters what they remember about that first day and chances are they'll say Spam sandwiches.

Kitty, at age two, was talking a blue streak. She had learned nursery rhymes from all of us, and Daddy had taught her songs he had learned from the Grand Ole Opry on the radio. She knew every word and never missed a note. She rode much of the way on Robert's lap in the cab, singing and keeping everyone entertained.

Back on the road, we passed through several small towns, and before darkness overtook us we saw a countryside splattered with low red hills. Then Daddy stopped and rented a tourist cabin for five dollars. We climbed out of the truck and looked up into a sky that was big and wide and filled with a million stars. Off in the distance a coyote howled as we hurried inside. The cabin was small, but everyone was tired and we managed in the two beds, with Mama and Daddy and the two babies in one, and Tink and me in the other with June, Judy, and Susie at our feet. The boys slept on the floor.

Before daylight, we were back on the road. We crossed the Texas border before breakfast. I was happily surprised when Mama told Robert to switch with me so I could ride in front for a few hours.

Old 66 was a straight shot across the Texas Panhandle. We passed through the center of every little town, and in between, it seemed you could see forever across the high plains. Mama read off the names of cities and towns to come, like Amarillo, Tucumcari, and Albuquerque. I tried to make sense of the Burma-Shave signs: She Kissed The Hairbrush/By Mistake/She Thought It Was/Her Husband Jake./Burma-Shave.

Mama had it all mapped out for Daddy. We were still in Texas when he asked her, "How far will we make it today?"

She said, "I think we can get to Tucumcari."

She was right. We rode past a strip of neon lights with everything from brightly lit teepees to bucking broncos and on out of the town. When at last Daddy pulled over and rented a small adobe cabin for the night, the lights of Tucumcari, New Mexico, were behind us.

The next day, after more small towns with strange names, we arrived in Albuquerque. I sat on the floor, my arms draped across one of the benches, and tried to pronounce the peculiar words on the signs. Words like La Mesa, El Vado, La Puerta, Azteca, Casa Grande. We were in a strange land. Then we left the city behind and chugged our way up a steep mountain grade. Daddy shifted gears and the truck jerked. We kids huddled together in the back and stared wide-eyed at the slanting road behind us. Sid called out, "Look! Live snakes." June, Judy, and Susie scampered back against the cab. Sid laughed and said, "Well, that's what the sign said."

Then we were in Gallup, New Mexico. It looked like one big trading post. All along the road there were tables and blankets laid out and covered with things for sale: Navajo rugs, Indian pottery, woolen blankets, leather purses, silver and turquoise jewelry. We didn't take time to look at anything. We were headed for the Arizona state line.

⁓

I was sitting on a bench in the back of the pickup, looking across the vast Arizona desert, when I heard a rattle underneath the truck and we coasted off onto the narrow shoulder of the road. Mama, Daddy, and Robert walked to the back of the truck and Robert lifted Kitty into the back with me. She stood wide-eyed and clung to the tailgate. I started to climb out too and Daddy said, "Stay where you are, all of you. We're parked too close to the road." Then he told Robert to get behind the wheel while he rolled the back tire off the pavement.

"What do you reckon it is, Daddy?" Mama's voice quivered.

"I don't have any ide'," he said. He lay on the ground and looked under the truck, but Daddy was no mechanic. He got up and said he'd have to go for help.

Mama was beside herself. "There's no tellin' how far you'll have to walk."

"Somebody'll pick me up."

"Look at that road. There ain't a car in sight."

"I'll go with him," Robert said.

"No, you won't," Daddy told him. "You stay here with Mama and the kids. We can't both leave them."

"Daddy, what if you don't get a ride?" Mama pleaded. "How long am I supposed to wait here? Something could happen to you."

"Ain't nothin' gonna happen to me."

"It's forty, maybe fifty miles into Holbrook, the next big town. And this is Saturday. You ain't gonna find nothin' between here and Holbrook except a few tradin' posts."

"Mama, we can't just set here. I gotta try to find help." And leaving Mama and the nine of us kids sitting beside the road, Daddy started hitch-hiking. After a few minutes a car passed. Before long there was another, and it passed, too. Robert tried to reassure Mama. "You'll see. Somebody will pick him up."

"Oh God," Mama said. "He's got all that money on him. Somebody could pick him up and kill him."

Daddy kept turning and waving back at us, as if to say, "I'm all right, I'll be back soon."

Ahead of him, the road curved and disappeared in the distance. Mama watched him walk farther away and said, "If he goes out of sight without gettin' a ride, I don't know what I'll do."

A pickup passed. Then the driver hit his brakes and pulled over. Daddy ran and climbed in the back. He stood up holding onto the cab, and waved his old brown Stetson hat at us as the truck rounded the curve and drove out of sight.

Mama sent the kids out into the open field away from the road to play. She sat in the cab with the door open as the rest of us, even Robert, went out into the desert to explore. Traffic was light, though, and she couldn't sit still for long. Soon she was pacing, watching the road in both directions, with the baby in her arms. Finally a tow truck came into sight and there was Daddy beside the driver. He had a big smile on his face.

"Oh, thank you, God," Mama said, wiping her tears with the back of her hand.

The pickup swayed back and forth as we eased down the highway behind the wrecker. After about ten miles we passed a long row of signs announcing Pottery, Indian Moccasins, Navajo Rugs, Steer Horns, Indian Paintings, and Clean Rest Rooms. The tow truck pulled into a small garage alongside a service station. Next to it was a trading post, and next to that, a row of white tourist cabins.

We were in Chambers, Arizona—one more family of Okies on our way to California, looking for a better life, and we were stuck. The truck had a broken axle and although there was a mechanic who could fix it, there wasn't any way to get parts until Monday. Mama was happy, though, because the cabin was comfortable. It only had one bed, but it had a nice bathroom and a kitchenette, and there were groceries for sale at the trading post. We kids slept with pillows all over the floor.

The next day, I wanted to go look at things in the trading post, but Mama said, "You know Daddy wouldn't like it if he caught you and Tink over there." She told us to watch the little kids and keep them close to the house, safe from the cars that were pulling in for gas.

Kitty played happily in the gravel. She filled the pocket of her dress with little rocks. Daddy stood just inside the door, looking out at the endless desert across the highway. "I hate settin' here like this for two whole days," he said. "Just waitin'."

"It ain't such a bad place, Daddy," Mama said. "The kids is doin' all right."

"I won't rest until we got a home again. That means we got to be on the road."

I spent most of my day right there on the steps, watching Robert and Sid across the way by the trading post. I wished I could be with them. Daddy was so worried and distracted, I didn't dare ask him. At least Mama was comfortable and content. She had a chance to rest, and it seemed to be just what she needed.

Monday morning at eleven, a Greyhound bus pulled in and a driver jumped off with a package. The mechanic met him and took the package, and the bus pulled away, leaving a cloud of dust behind. Our part had arrived.

While the truck was being worked on, Daddy spent most of his time at the garage, and I sneaked inside the trading post. I looked at pretty hand-tooled leather purses hanging on pegs behind the counter. Inside a glass case were turquoise bead necklaces and silver belt buckles. I walked around, not looking too closely for fear I'd get caught. There were a few Indians in the store. Their hair hung down their backs in long black braids, even the men's, and they wore colorful blankets over their shoulders. I didn't hear them say anything. I only stayed a few minutes and then I ran to the cabin to tell Tink what I had seen, but she was helping Mama with the dishes, so I kept my secret.

The truck was ready that afternoon and Daddy was anxious to get back on the road, so we pulled out and headed across the desert toward Holbrook. When we got there, Daddy nosed the truck into a space between two parked cars. Mama told me to come with her. Daddy fed pennies into a meter and said, "We got twenty minutes, Mama."

I followed her past a long plate-glass window with a display of beautifully dressed mannequins. She opened the door and we stepped inside what seemed to me to be a big department store.

Someone said, "Can I help you?"

Mama said, "I'm lookin' for a coat for her," nodding toward me.

The clerk led us across the store to a round rack of new winter coats. Mama shuffled past everything until she found a deep red.

After she checked the size and the price, she took it off the rack and said to me, "Slip your arms in here." I wrapped the coat around me. It was warm and soft.

"Step over here," the lady said. I looked into the full-length mirror. Blue was my favorite color, and Tink's was pink. It was Mama who loved red, so when she asked me if I liked it, I said I did.

It was red with black buttons, and a perfect fit. I had never owned such a pretty coat, and I did like it. Mama smiled as she watched me turning and looking at myself in the mirror. "It won't be so cold where we're goin'. Not like Oklahoma. But you'll need a new coat for school. That one's pretty, and not too heavy for California weather." She turned to the clerk and said, "We'll take it."

I walked out of the store wearing my new coat. Mama said, "Hurry, baby, Daddy's waitin' and he don't want to lose too much time."

As I rushed down the street, I saw him leaning on the door of the truck with the window down. Sid and Robert were on the edge of the curb, standing beside the parking meter. Sid was bent over with laughter. Daddy and Robert were both focused on Sid, and it was easy to see they were both getting a kick out of him.

I said, "Are you laughin' at my red coat?"

"What? Your coat?" Sid looked me up and down. "That ain't funny. That's pretty." He hunched his shoulders and motioned me closer to him. "Listen at them guys down on the corner." He covered his mouth to muffle a laugh. "Don't they talk funny? They talk so fast, I don't see how they keep up with each other."

The men were speaking a different language than we did. They had dark skin, but they weren't Indians. They were small in stature. They were having a good time, laughing.

Mama said, "They must be from Old Mexico. It's just across the border near here."

"Listen to them," Sid went on. "What's that they're talkin' anyway?"

"Well, if they're from Mexico, I reckon they talk Mexican, don't they?" Robert said.

There we were, kids fresh off an Oklahoma farm, on the streets of Holbrook, Arizona, hearing Spanish for the first time. The men, a few feet away, paid no attention to us at all.

Daddy looked at Mama and both of them laughed. Then Daddy said, "Let's go. I want to get to Flagstaff before it's too late." Mama put my coat in a bag and carefully tucked it behind the seat, where it wouldn't get dirty.

⤳

That evening, after five days on the road, we left the high sunlit desert and drove into the mountains of northern Arizona. Traces of snow lay beside the road. We huddled under our quilts and the babies slept. Finally, the lights of Flagstaff spread out before us. Again I watched the road behind the truck. Snowflakes fell through the air, dancing in the neon lights. Downtown was lit with every color of the rainbow. Red proclaimed NO VACANCY. Other signs advertising pancakes, fried chicken, and Chinese and Mexican food lined both sides of Old 66. I have seen the lights of many big cities, but none stand out so vividly in my memory as those I saw from the back of a pickup truck on a cold November night in Flagstaff, Arizona.

On the far end of town, we found a vacancy sign and stopped for the night. Tall pine trees were new to us. Their limbs hung like wide green brushes beside the cabins, and they bent toward the ground under the weight of snow.

⤳

We left Flagstaff in the early morning darkness and drove only a few miles when the truck sputtered a couple of times. Daddy steered it, coasting, off the road, saying, "We must be outta gas! How could I have forgot the gas!"

There we were again, with no town in sight and Daddy set to take off walking back to town. It was still dark, and Mama was pleading for him to wait for daylight. Daddy said, "What was I thinkin'? Why didn't I fill up last night?"

"You was lookin' for a place to spend the night, that's why," Mama said.

Daddy was so anxious. We were already two days late, and he knew Aunt Addie was expecting us and probably worrying.

Headlights came into sight. The car slowed down but drove on by. Then it turned around, came back, and stopped next to us. A man rolled down his window and said, "You folks got trouble?"

"Outta gas," Robert said. "Daddy forgot to fill up."

"Looks like you got a load."

Daddy laughed. "Mostly kids. We're movin' to California. I got three sisters there. This is supposed to be our last day on the road, but we ain't gettin' there very fast like this." Now Daddy and the man both laughed.

"Hop in," the man said, "and we'll take you back to Flagstaff. We ought to be able to find something open."

So once again, Daddy left us all sitting beside the road. Robert got in the cab beside Mama. "You sleepy?" he asked her.

"Son, I don't know if I'll ever get caught up. I'm awful tired. It's gonna be midnight or after when we get to Addie's house tonight. Are the other kids asleep?"

Everyone was except Robert and me.

A few cars passed. Robert leaned back on the seat. Mama told me to go try to get some sleep. I held on to the pickup bed and waded the slippery snow. The forest felt close and dark and lonely. I squeezed in with the other kids and pulled covers over me, but I couldn't sleep. I thought about my new red coat tucked away in a sack behind the seat. I couldn't wait to wear it. I thought about California. I wanted to ask Mama how long it would be before we reached the state line.

The lights of a car filled the pickup bed and brought me back to earth. I sat up when I heard Daddy's voice, and the headlights blinded me. I held my hands in front of my face.

Daddy had a five-gallon can of gas. The man, still laughing and talking to Daddy, helped get the truck going, and he wished us a safe trip. Daddy shook his hand and said, "You don't have no ide' what you've done for us, drivin' all the way back out here. I can't thank you enough."

The man said how much he enjoyed meeting Daddy. Walking back to his car, he called out to us, "Lots of luck to you!"

Daddy answered, "God bless ya'."

ↄ

Daylight came through the trees in Kaibab National Forest as we left the snow behind. At Williams, signs pointed to the Grand Canyon. Ahead lay the Black Mountains and, beyond them, the Mojave Desert. After we stopped for breakfast, I sat in the back of the pickup enjoying my sweet roll, watching for a glimpse of the canyon. We crossed high plains with sagebrush and ranch land, and passed through more towns and Indian reservations. I had hardly become used to the sight of pine trees when we came upon tall cactuses with thick arms reaching toward the sky.

We were about to begin our treacherous climb through the Black Mountains when Daddy stopped to make sure we all were safe. He secured the tailgate and said, "Better set on the floor, kids." The stretch of windy road with its hairpin curves was the steepest part of all. I rested my arm on one of the benches and looked down on sharp curves behind us. The higher we climbed, the steeper and more dangerous the grade became. Sid said, "Look, a burned-up truck." I looked over an embankment and sure enough, far below, the remains of a charred pickup rested at the bottom of a gorge. We clung to Mama's beautiful benches while she watched us through the window of the cab. It was a long dangerous passage, but I knew our parents would carry us to safety.

Then the road started to descend, still twisting and turning around the mountains until at last we reached the tiny old Gold Rush town of Oatman. It was a welcome sight, with its weather-beaten buildings. The red rocks surrounding the town stood out against the blue sky. Daddy drove past an old hotel and the shops and bars, and kept right on going. Maneuvering the truck along the curves that led down to the Colorado River, Daddy rode his brakes, but, compared to the mountain behind us, this drive was easy. At the bottom, a long bridge crossed the Colorado River. On the other side, the town of Needles awaited us.

༄

Tall palms trees decorated the small desert town. Motels and coffee shops lined Route 66. Before starting across the Mojave Desert, Daddy filled up again with gas and bought food. He put the lunch sack on the floor by us. "I know it's late," he said, "but don't open anythin' in here before we stop."

As soon as we were on the road, Susie pulled a Pepsi out of the sack. Sid reached for the bottle.

"I ain't gonna open it," she said. "I'm just gonna hold it." She shook the bottle and the Pepsi fizzed. We all laughed and she shook it again.

"Faster!" Sid said. "Shake it faster." With a big smile, Susie shook it as fast as her five-year-old arms would go. There was a loud Pop! and the lid blew into the air, spraying soda pop all over the back of the pickup. Sid ducked too late, and the top of his head was covered with cold Pepsi-Cola. Susie's black eyes were big as saucers. Her face was a mass of white foam that ran out over both hands, trickled down her arms, and soaked the front of her dress. We were roaring with laughter as Daddy pulled off the road for our lunch stop.

It was November 4, 1947, a warm, sunny day, as I climbed over the tailgate, slid down the back of the pickup, and set my feet for the first time on California soil.

ॐ

We reached the agricultural check-in station at Barstow in the dark. Daddy walked to the back of the pickup. A man dressed in uniform shone a flashlight in my face. He asked Daddy where he was headed and what he had in the back of the truck. He was pleasant and friendly as he shone the light over all of us. He said, "Man, you have a pickup full of pretty girls. Why don't you give me one?"

"Which one would you like to have?" Daddy said, and laughed.

"I'll take that one with the big blue eyes," he said.

Judy grabbed June's hand and dragged her into the far corner of the pickup. Daddy and the man laughed, and Daddy tried to tell the twins he was only teasing, but they didn't come out of their corner until we were back on the road.

From Barstow, Route 66 headed toward Los Angeles. After two thousand miles on that familiar road, it was time to leave it. We would be at Aunt Addie's house in time to bed down late that night.

Only, the next morning, I woke up as the pickup bounced off the blacktop and pulled into a service station. Daddy told me we were in Barstow—again.

Mama had tears in her eyes. "It's all right, honey. I'm just tired. When we left here last night, we took the right road but we went the wrong direction."

"We drove all night?"

"Yeah," Robert said, "at midnight last night, we was about to cross into Nevada." He smiled.

"Ain't nothin' funny about it, son," Mama said. "Me and Daddy lost a night's sleep. We're dead tired and we still got a day's drive ahead of us."

Then, as if things weren't bad enough, Daddy rushed back to the pickup and said, "I can't find my wallet!"

"Ain't it in your back pocket?"

"No, Mama. I looked. I ain't got it on me."

I put Kitty in the back and took Jimmy in my arms while Mama and Robert looked everywhere with Daddy. Under the seat, behind the seat. They pulled out the seat bottom. Mama dumped her purse, even though she knew it wasn't there.

Daddy helped her push the seat back into place. "Let me think," he said. He rested his forehead on his arms.

"You paid for gas last night, Daddy. You had your wallet then?"

"No, I had money in my shirt pocket. You know I don't carry all the money in one place. But I keep most of it in my wallet, every dime we got in the world. I kept it separate, and that wallet's gone. We got two hundred miles to go, a bunch of hungry kids, and I got a couple dollars in change in my pocket."

"Did you put it in one of them grocery sacks? Think a minute, Daddy. When did you have it last?"

"I gave you money to buy Betty's coat. I kept out enough to buy gas and somethin' to eat. I ain't seen it since then. But I know I put it in my back pocket."

"Did you see it in Flagstaff?"

Daddy thought for a few seconds. Then a big smile crossed his face. "That's it! Flagstaff. I put them khaki pants on under my overalls." He unfastened the bib of his overalls and they dropped to the ground. He reached into the back pocket of his khakis and out came his wallet. His lips quivered and tears came to his eyes.

"For goodness' sakes," Mama said. "Why did you put them khakis on?"

"That extra pair of pants felt pretty good with snow on the ground," Daddy said, "but I plum forgot I had 'em on. Now get back in the pickup. I'll pay for this gas and then get something for us to eat, and I ain't stoppin' again until we get to Addie's house."

~

The last day of our journey, I sat in the back of the truck and watched the road snake its way through the Tehachapi Mountains. The narrow, steep grade was more frightening than Northern Arizona, as we hugged the road only inches from a drop-off. My first glance over the edge, I felt as if I were being sucked toward the bottom. There were no guardrails. One bobble and we would have rolled forever over the canyon walls. Other automobiles skimmed the side of the mountain behind us.

I've heard families from Oklahoma and Arkansas talk about the first time they saw the San Joaquin Valley from two thousand feet above sea level high in the Tehachapi Mountains. Many of them stopped and gazed at the fields, groves, and vineyards. They got out of their cars and yelled and danced and waved their arms. Many laughed and cried and hugged one another.

Mama, Daddy, and Robert saw the San Joaquin Valley for the first time through the dusty windshield of our 1938 Ford pickup. Mama later told me, "We was too tired to do any shoutin'." But as Daddy began our descent, she heard him say, "Dear Lord, please help. I've got some important cargo in the back."

Partway down the mountain we came upon an accident. A car pulling a trailer had jack-knifed and was hit by another car. A wrecker was at the scene, leaving barely enough room for us to pass.

At last we reached the bottom, and Bakersfield came into sight. There were fewer than sixty miles between us and a good night's sleep. Safe on Aunt Addie's floor, I would close my eyes that night and drift off with visions of deep canyons and perilous mountain roads in front of my face.

CALIFORNIA

Corcoran

SHORTLY AFTER THREE O'CLOCK in the afternoon, we turned off Central Valley Highway and drove across the railroad tracks, past the old train depot, and into the dusty little farming town of Corcoran, California. Tiny particles of cotton floated in the air and a strange, unfamiliar odor burned my nose. I wondered how long it had been since the last good rain.

As we drove down Whitley Avenue, the main thoroughfare, we saw trucks pulling long trailers filled with cotton making their way through town. The sides of the trailers were lined with chicken wire, and the cotton was packed tightly. Locks of cotton blew from the trailers onto the street, and, caught by the breeze from the traffic, they landed in the gutters and lay there gathering dust among the candy wrappers and cigarette butts.

We turned down a side street and followed it, searching for Aunt Addie's house. At the far edge of town, we came upon a big cotton gin. The bale yard covered several acres and was filled with tall rectangular bundles of cotton. Each tightly packed bale was wrapped with strips of brown burlap and tied with long strands of wire. The tops of each of the bales protruded like huge powder puffs standing on the ground in long rows behind a cyclone fence. A sign at the entrance read "J.G. Boswell Co." We later learned that Boswell was the world's largest corporate farmer and that Corcoran was home to Boswell's biggest gin. This was our new home.

Aunt Addie's house on Hall Avenue was locked. No one

answered the door and the place looked deserted. Daddy said every-one was probably in the fields. It was November 5, and along the house, Aunt Addie's roses were still in bloom. I spotted a garden hose stretched across the grass and everyone fell in line behind me. After quenching our thirst, we sat on the steps and waited.

The babies played on the grass, but Mama and Daddy were care-ful to keep them away from the streets. In about thirty minutes, Vir-ginia, our twelve-year-old cousin, came prancing down the sidewalk with her baton. She ran to Daddy and hugged him and said, "You're late, Uncle Bill. Mama expected you three days ago."

She showed us around, and Mama noticed a fruit tree she hadn't seen before. Virginia said it had nectarines, a sweet white fruit. "Sort of like a peach," she said, "only without the fuzz." She was friendly and bubbly, and helped cheer us up. I heard the sound of drums and horns and I rushed out into the yard and then to the sidewalk. The Corcoran Union High School band was marching down the middle of Hall Avenue straight toward me. A teenage boy led them, pranc-ing and twirling his baton. Two pretty majorettes behind him kept perfect time, showing off their long legs. They came within two houses of me, then turned down a side street and circled back toward the school a couple of blocks away.

My cousin came out with her baton, twirling it as well as the girls who had just passed. She showed me how to move the baton under my arm and over the outside of my hand. I could make it twirl, but not like Virginia.

It was almost dark when Aunt Addie and Uncle Ivan came home from the field. Daddy cried and hugged his sister. "You look tired," he said.

"She ought to be," Uncle Ivan said. "She picked almost five hun-dred pounds today."

Daddy laughed. "And how much did you pick?"

"I don't pick. I run the crew. I weigh the cotton and stamp the tickets. I even got a man hired to empty sacks for the women and the kids." Uncle Ivan went on to say that it would be Christmas before the cotton was gone. There was work for all of us.

After dinner, the house filled with aunts and cousins as Daddy and his three sisters reminisced about their parents, whom they had lost at a young age. On the living room wall hung a black-and-white photograph in an oval frame with a bubble glass front. Their father was seated. Their mother, with long black hair, stood tall beside her husband in a long dress with lots of white lace. Aunt Addie pointed to the photograph and said, "Bill, I never noticed it before tonight, but Betty looks like our mother." I knew how they loved and missed her. The suggestion that I might be like her in any way made me proud.

I sat glued to the floor as they talked about the few years they all spent together after losing both their parents. I knew Daddy was only nine when his mother died. That night at Aunt Addie's house, she began the whole story again: "The last time we saw our mother conscious, she tucked us into bed." It was like a myth to me, this story, and maybe it was to them, too, one they had to tell over and over again to keep the memories alive.

Daddy said, "When I went to sleep, she was settin' on our dad's lap and she was laughin'. The next thing I knowed, he woke me. My mama was unconscious. He lit the kerosene lantern and sent me for a doctor. There was a big snow on the ground. I don't know how I found my way. I remember wadin' snow and carryin' that lantern across the railroad track." He said that when he finally found the doctor and got back home, his mama still didn't know anyone. She died three days later, on Christmas Eve. She had bad headaches, "catarrh," the doctor called them. But who knows? She might have had a brain tumor.

Aunt Addie said, "You can't know what it's like to a child who loses their mother unless you've been one. And when our daddy died a few years later, we was just four little orphans, but we was determined to stay together."

Daddy told us about how he went into town a few days before their dad died and made funeral arrangements. He said, "The cemetery was on the other side of the river, and the four of us kids rode across in Ernest Dinsmore's wagon with our daddy's body in a pine box I had bought, just like he had told me to do."

"I don't know how we survived and stayed together," Aunt Ida said. "Times was hard and I was so little."

Daddy said, "I took work wherever I could find it. We done without a lot, but we made it."

"Remember that awful flood," she said.

Uncle Ivan said, "It had rained for days, causing flood waters everywhere. We was outta food, so Bill and me decided to cross Grand River in a drift boat and go to town."

Aunt Ida told how the little kids begged Daddy not to go because he couldn't swim. Sure enough, before he and Uncle Ivan reached the other side, the boat overturned, and there was Ivan clinging to a drift, while they thought Daddy had drowned.

Daddy turned to Uncle Ivan and laughed, "I was OK 'til you run that water snake out over me. I was scared to death of snakes."

Aunt Ida said, "We was on the bank searching the river for some sign of you, when we saw your hat wavin' above the drift. We kept watchin' for that old hat 'til help got there."

"Yeah," Daddy said, "Times was hard, but here we are. We made it."

And there we all were, gathered at Aunt Addie's house. Aunts, uncles, cousins, two thousand miles from where the story began. Happily, even Uncle Clinton was there. He had followed Aunt Ida and their kids to Corcoran and they remarried about a month before we arrived.

The search for a house was useless. The town was full of migrant workers and nothing was available, not even a cabin or a tent in the labor camps. After Daddy and Mama had spent most of a day searching, Mama came home upset about the conditions some people were living in. She said, "We saw people livin' under that old bridge south of town."

Uncle Ivan told her, "That's the way it is here every fall, Elsie. People move on soon as the work runs out, though." He assured them they would find a house once the cotton was all picked, in a month or two. Daddy worried he'd made the wrong decision. We had had our Oklahoma place rented through December, and he wondered if we should have stayed, but Uncle Ivan reminded him that he wouldn't have wanted to bring us across the mountains in the dead of winter. "Best thing to do is keep your eyes and ears open in the field. Somebody will be movin' and you'll hear about it."

"Ain't nothin' else we can do, I reckon," Daddy said. It was hard for my parents. They wanted us to have a home of our own.

Early Saturday morning, we followed Uncle Ivan to the fields while Mama stayed home with the babies. Two miles west of town we entered the cotton fields of the Tulare Lake Basin. Within minutes, we were surrounded by a sea of fluffy cotton that swallowed us up as Uncle Ivan drove deeper into the fertile fields. The next thing I knew, the pickup pulled up a steep slope and we followed his car atop a wide levee. I looked down on an irrigation ditch of shallow, murky water. We passed several crews. Empty trailers sat on the edge of the fields waiting to be filled, and there were other partly filled trailers that had been left overnight. I wondered how so much cotton could ever be brought into the gin.

Uncle Ivan left the levee and parked on the edge of the field where several early birds from his crew were already working. We all piled out of the pickup, and Daddy gave Robert, Tink, and me each a new six-foot, canvas cotton sack he had bought at Rio Grande Market the day before. He pulled the strap of his sack over his head and hung it across his shoulder. Bunching it up and tucking it under his arm, he headed down between two rows of cotton and we all followed.

At the end of the field, I put my own sack over my shoulder and let it drag on the ground. To the west, there was cotton as far as the eye could see. To the north and south, there was more of the same all the way to the horizon. I didn't know there was that much cotton in the whole world—the most beautiful cotton I had ever seen. On the east side of the valley, about eighty miles away, the snow-capped Sierra Nevada stood out against a bright blue sky.

Daddy gave us instructions about where to work, keeping Susie close to him. I grabbed handfuls of cotton and crammed them into my sack, amazed at how fast it filled up. I picked up the cotton that June piled on the ground, and cleaned up the ragged stalks she left behind. (Tink was doing the same with Judy.) Then I lifted the sack and shook it hard, sending the cotton into the bottom of my sack.

We worked for about an hour, and then the babies complained that they were thirsty. Daddy said, "We all need a drink. Besides that, we better go to the scales before our sacks get too heavy." More cotton than we could keep dragging, after only an hour—this was a first!

A line had formed at the scales, and I waited with the load dangling across my back. The heavy sack tugged at the muscles in my neck, and I put my hand on my hip to brace the load. If I dropped it on the ground, I would have to drag it to the front of the line and pick it up again. What a relief it was when I finally backed up to the scales and Uncle Ivan reached under my sack with a chain, wrapped it around the sack, hung it on the scales, and I was free to step out from under the load. He stamped a ticket with the number of pounds, minus three pounds for the sack.

"Don't lose this," he warned. "It's the same as money. We cash them every Saturday, and if you lose your tickets, you don't get paid." Daddy took tickets from all of us and put them in his wallet.

Beside the scales a partly filled trailer was parked. It had a ladder on each side and a couple of wide boards across the top. Daddy shouldered his sacks and climbed the ladder, with Robert following behind him. At the top, Daddy stepped from the ladder onto one of the boards and walked a few feet out. Reaching back, he pulled a string that released the cotton from the bottom of his sack. Cotton emptied out of both ends and dropped into the trailer.

Sacks full of cotton lay all over the ground as Aunt Addie waited in line for hers to be emptied. After he had dumped mine and Tink's, Daddy shouldered Aunt Addie's and started up the ladder. Uncle Ivan said, "Don't do that, Bill. That's what my helper gets paid for." But Daddy was already atop the trailer. Meanwhile, Aunt Ida put her load across her shoulder and started for the ladder, too. Daddy called to her to put the sack down before she got hurt.

She laughed. "Oh, I can empty my own sack. I'm tough."

"You ain't that tough. Don't be foolish."

"I'm all right, Bill. I've done this before." She climbed the ladder and Daddy moved out of her way as she stepped onto the board. He climbed down the other side, grumbling, "You ain't got no business up there, Ida. You've always been a stubborn woman. There's some things women just don't do."

As we started back to work, Daddy turned to Tink and me and said, "Don't ever try to dump your own sack, no matter how long you have to wait. Let men do that kind a stuff. They're stronger. And besides that, it ain't decent."

A big truck turned into the field and drove past us slowly. Our cousin Floyd smiled and waved. He backed in and lined the truck up with a full cotton trailer, got out, and hooked the trailer to the truck, then pulled it away.

Robert said, "Daddy, if I drop outta school, Floyd said he can get me a job with him. I can make a lot more money drivin' a truck than I can pickin' cotton."

"No, son. You only got one more year of school. There'll be plenty a time for work. I don't want you to quit school."

Robert knew not to argue with Daddy.

At noon, about half the crew went home. We stopped for lunch, then worked until midafternoon. By then most everyone was leaving to cash their cotton tickets. Finally Uncle Ivan called everyone in for the day. We weighed up one last time and followed Uncle Ivan into town.

Rio Grande Market cashed tickets for Uncle Ivan's crew. Daddy gave each of us half of what we made that day. He kept the rest, saying that he would save it for things we would need in the winter, like shoes. That would be the rule for the duration of our life in the cotton fields.

I didn't know how tired I was until we got home. The field had been hot and dirty and I needed a bath, but what I wanted most was to lie down across Mama's bed and rest. Dinner didn't even sound good. I had weighed up almost two hundred pounds of cotton. My shoulder was raw from pulling a heavy load all day, and by evening every bone in my body ached.

Then I started thinking about Tiawah. I thought about the new basketball jackets that had been ordered for our team. I hadn't seen them because I left before they arrived. I wondered who would get mine. I felt sick inside, knowing I was no longer a part of that team. I missed my friends. I wanted to be able to walk out to the barn lot with Wanda and Lola and skate on the ice. What had I been thinking of? A day like this?

We were crowded up in Aunt Addie's house, sleeping wherever we could. I'd just picked more cotton than I ever had in my life. I was too tired to eat. This wasn't what Mama and I had dreamed of. But maybe it wouldn't be like this for long. Daddy would find a house for us, and things might get better.

Enrolled

WE HAD TO STAY IN SCHOOL until we were sixteen, and truant officers patrolled the fields as regularly as immigration officers. If school-age children were found working during the week, their parents had to pay a stiff fine. Robert was sixteen, though, and all day Sunday he pleaded with Daddy to allow him to drop out and work.

Daddy was torn. "We never even talked about this," he said. "It was always understood, our kids would graduate." He and Mama agonized over it, but to my surprise, on Monday morning, as the rest of us dressed for school, Robert went to work with Floyd.

Mama walked the twins and Sid to Brett Harte Grammar School, named for the famous writer of stories of the California Gold Rush and other Western fiction. The school couldn't hold all the students, with the town full of migrant workers, so classes had been set up in several churches. The school people sent Mama and her three kids to the Grange Hall first. Sid was enrolled there, and then Mama went on to the Methodist Church with the twins. The teachers wanted to move Judy up a grade, but Mama wouldn't hear of it. She said, "This is gonna be hard enough. They ain't never been separated, and I don't want to do it now."

I was wearing my new red coat when I walked through the big swinging doors of Corcoran Union High School. To the left was a long winding staircase, and down the hall, rows of lockers. Students were rushing to first-period class, as locker doors slammed. The jun-

*Kitty, 1947, seated on the 1938 Ford pickup the Grants
drove to California.*

Aunt Ada, Uncle Leonard, and family, 1930s.

*Grandma and Granpa Bristol, Pittsburg, California, in front of the fish
cannery where they worked, 1948.*

Betty with guitar, Dairy Avenue, 1948.

Mama's morning glory vines, Dairy Avenue, 1949.

Jim, Beth and Julie Proctor, and Kitty, Dairy Avenue, 1949.

Tink, Dairy Avenue, 1949.

*Betty, graduation day, Dairy
Avenue, 1950.*

Daddy and Mama, Dairy Avenue, 1951.

Betty weeding cotton, August 1951. Her friend Robert dropped by on his way to Korea.

Betty in sombrero, 1952.

Sid, Judy, Susie, June, Jimmy, and Kitty, 1952.

Daddy and one of his quarter horses, 1967.

ior high and high school were all in one big building, almost a thousand students, and I didn't know anyone.

I went through the door marked Admitting Office. A tall, frail-looking woman leaned toward me across the counter. Her cheekbones seemed to push against the skin of her thin face and her eyes sank back into her head behind black-rimmed glasses. Her hair was piled on top of her head. Looking at me, she growled, "Are you here to enroll?"

A chill swept over me as I nodded and answered, "Uh-huh."

"Uh-huh? What kind of word is that? Didn't anyone teach you to say, 'Yes, ma'am'?" She reached under the counter and shoved a stack of papers toward me. "Fill these out. Print. OK? Print."

Tink and our cousin Louise stepped up beside me. "You go on to class," the thin woman said. "No need for you to go dragging in late just because these kids do." Louise gave Tink a list of her classes and left.

Three other students walked in. I recognized two sisters I had met on the field Saturday, Joyce and Helen Crawford. I asked them if they were starting school, too.

"We just moved here from McCallister," Joyce said. Meeting someone from Oklahoma was like finding kin.

"Where are you stayin'?" I asked.

"We got relatives. We're livin' in a tent on their place."

"My daddy looked everywhere. There ain't no place to rent. We're staying with my aunt."

A pretty blond girl I remembered from the field was standing beside Joyce. She introduced herself. "I'm Norma." I offered her one of the papers to fill out, but she said she had enrolled a month earlier.

I asked her where she lived. She said, "We always stay in the Green Camp."

"What do you mean, 'always'?"

"We don't live here. Our home's in Tennessee. We leave there every summer and follow the work. Usually, when cotton season ends, we head for home. My daddy said we might go to Lindsay and pick oranges this year. I hope not. I wanna go home."

I remembered her daddy from the field. "That tall man that keeps everyone laughin.' The one everbody calls Tennessee. My daddy said it's important to have a guy like Tennessee in the fields. He makes hardworkin' people forget their troubles."

The lady with the black glasses picked up her purse and said, "Enough chatter. You're all late for class." Then she left out the back door.

The school secretary was nicer and more helpful. She got Tink into the classes she was hoping for. Joyce and I headed for the gym and first-period P.E.

Miss Edison had already called roll. She took Joyce and me into her office to give us a list of the things we would need for class. I had tennis shoes, but when she told us we would have to buy gym shorts at the Mercantile store, and that we were required to dress out every day in order to pass, my heart sank.

When we were out of the office, I asked Joyce, "Does your daddy let you wear shorts?"

She laughed. "He don't like it. But when I tell him it's required, he'll have to let me. Are you worried about your daddy?"

"Yeah. He's gonna have a fit. He ain't never let me wear them before. Not even to play basketball in a tournament."

"You ain't got no other choice," she said. "It ain't your fault. We have to dress out every day or we can't graduate."

It was one of the most traumatic days of my life as I went from class to class, not knowing anyone. I sat near the back in almost every classroom. When the final bell rang, I forgot all about my new red coat, tucked away in my locker. I hurried down the stairs and out the door, and ran three blocks home to the safety of Aunt Addie's home.

That night at dinner, I had to tell Daddy about having to wear the gym shorts, and at first he said I would do no such thing. Aunt Addie explained that it was required, but Daddy kept saying girls were different. Aunt Addie argued that with six daughters, Daddy was going to have to get used to some new ways. Finally Uncle Ivan said, "It's no use, Bill, you can't argue with a doorknob! You have to set different rules for girls. But the school's got you on this one. Besides, remember, it's only one hour a day, and it's inside with a bunch of other girls."

Daddy finally agreed, saying, "Don't ever let me catch you wearin' shorts anywhere else!" I looked across at Mama. She smiled and glanced down at her plate.

The next day, Tink, Joyce, Helen, and I walked down to the Mercantile during our lunch hour. We bought the required blue, one-piece, baggy gym outfit that belted at the waist and gathered on our thighs into bloomers. Tink and I had different class periods, so we only had to buy one outfit; we shared one locker and one pair of shoes, too.

We walked back to school, all of us glad that we would be just like all the other girls. We were walking along, not saying anything, and I suppose Tink got to wondering just where it was that Norma was from, because out of nowhere she asked, "Norma, where's Tennessee?"

"Oh, he's workin'. He's pickin' cotton," Norma said.

Tink and I burst into laughter and then Norma realized what Tink had meant. The three of us laughed until our sides hurt as we crossed the street and staggered into the school yard.

In the years that followed, I was always happy when Mama and Daddy came home from the field and announced, "Tennessee and his family are back." Then, during picking season, the year after I graduated from high school, they didn't show up.

Uncle Leonard

ONE SATURDAY MORNING, Mama left Jimmy and Kitty with one of our older cousins and went to the field with the rest of us. Five-year-old Susie followed Mama down the rows.

June was helping me and I was several yards ahead of Mama, so I turned back to help her catch up. When I reached her, I saw that she had been crying. "What is it, Mama? Do you miss home too?"

"No, honey, I hope we don't ever go back to Oklahoma. It's that I miss our babies. I ain't ever left any of my babies before. I oughta be breast-feedin' Jimmy right now. But he had to be put on a bottle before we left home 'cause of that swellin' in my breast. I'm afraid the little feller thinks I forsook him. I'm thankful for the work, but I'll be glad when the season ends. Maybe Daddy can find a job driving a tractor."

"I wish he could find a house," I said.

"Oh my, yes. I'd live in a tent a while, just to be out to ourselves."

We didn't have to resort to that. We lived with Aunt Addie's family for a month. Then one day Daddy carried his sack to the scales and came back for Mama's with a big smile on his face. "Are you ready for some good news?" he said. Uncle Ivan had introduced him to a man who was taking his family back to Arkansas the next week. He and Mama could look at their house that very night. The old three-room house was in Mitchell's labor camp, and it rented for thirty-five dollars a month. Daddy's sister, Aunt Ada, lived with her family in a one-room cabin in the same camp during picking season.

For most of the year, they lived in Brentwood, two hundred miles north in the San Francisco Bay area.

Aunt Ada was a sweet, kind woman, gentle with her six kids, and seemed to accept whatever came her way. She was about five feet, two inches tall. She picked cotton, but she didn't try to compete with her two sisters, who picked twice as much as she did.

Her husband, Uncle Leonard, was over six feet tall, and he towered over her. When he entered the kitchen as she was preparing a meal, and stepped in behind her, wrapping his long arms around her, she disappeared behind him. He was a striking figure, with a mass of red hair, and a real talker; he was what you would call an honest-to-goodness character. He drank too much, and often when he did he ended up in jail. When their son was killed in an automobile accident, he couldn't make it to the funeral because he was in Folsom prison for writing bad checks.

Yet Uncle Leonard could be a good worker, and Daddy often said he could get a job when no one else could. He proved it that fall of 1947, when Boswell Company brought in the first mechanical cotton picker to the Tulare Lake Basin on an experimental basis. Over a hundred men applied to drive that first picker, and no one was surprised when Uncle Leonard was hired. But then his family was hit by disaster that he couldn't handle.

A few days after we arranged to move into the camp, Aunt Ada's cabin burned. They lost everything except what they were wearing; they were out of the cabin at the time. Even Mama suffered a loss. Aunt Ada had been storing Mama's precious little rocking chair in the cabin, and it burned with the rest of the house.

That whole family, including six more cousins, crowded into Aunt Addie's house to sleep on the floor with us that night, and in the morning, Uncle Leonard loaded them into his old jalopy and headed back to Brentwood. He didn't even bother to go to the field to explain why he wouldn't be finishing out the season on the new picker. He just didn't show up.

Uncle Leonard wasn't a mean drunk, and, mostly, he kept his drinking to the weekends. But sometimes he got drunk and disappeared. He could drop out of sight for weeks or months. He might show up after hitching a ride to Oklahoma and back. Finally, one day he left, never to come back again. No one ever heard from him.

The sad thing to me about Uncle Leonard is that in spite of everything, there seemed to be so much love between him and my Aunt Ada. They were affectionate and she seemed to understand his restless spirit. In time, though, his children—not Aunt Ada—grew tired of putting up with him.

For a long time, Ada thought he would come back. All the kids grew up and left home, and still he hadn't returned. Then she gave him up for dead. She wondered if his body might be among the farm workers in the Juan Corona mass murder case, but she didn't check. She seemed to resign herself to the fact that Uncle Leonard's body was probably among the nameless graves in a potter's field somewhere.

Dairy Avenue

THE PICKUP KICKED UP a cloud of dust as we pulled off the blacktop on Dairy Avenue. Daddy opened the door of the truck and stepped down into the yard. He stood looking at the old house and said, "It ain't much, but I've lived in worse, and for now, it's home."

It looked like a deserted shell. Weather had stripped away the coat of whitewash except for a few streaks of white against the bare boards. The old hull had been hauled in and plunked down in the sand with no foundation.

Sid jumped out into the dirt and dusted the sand from his pants legs. Daddy told him, "Grab an armload and carry it to the house."

Mama carried Jimmy and climbed the rickety wooden steps. I followed her onto a small screened-in porch that led into a long narrow middle room. There stood a little gas range. I said, "Is that our cookstove?"

Daddy said, "I bought it from the Browns. And a little gas heater in the other room, too. Mama and me will go to the secondhand store after while and pick up some beds."

Later that day, he replaced the screen above the stove with Flex-O-Glass, which looked a lot like a regular screen but was made of plastic. It kept out the cold and let in the light, but we couldn't see out. He placed it over the screen on the front porch, also. Before the day was over, he had set up a bed on the porch for Robert and Sid.

There were two larger rooms, one on either side of the kitchen. One had two full-size beds for the six of us girls. The other was used as a living room as well as a bedroom for Mama, Daddy, and the baby. In one corner of our bedroom, Mama drove nails and stretched wire to make a place to hang our clothes. That evening when we gathered around the table and took our places on Mama's benches, we got a feeling of home.

There was no indoor plumbing. A gray outhouse sat at a slant in the sand in the backyard. In the middle of the camp was a community shower, off-limits to us girls unless Mama was with us. Tink and I showered at school after P.E. Other than that, bathing took place in a washtub. Mama was thankful for the luxuries of electricity and the gas stove. A cord hung from an open lightbulb on the ceiling. All we had to do was pull the cord to get light in the room. She said, "I ain't never cooked with anything but wood before. Gas is dangerous. It's an explosive, so be careful." And she showed Tink and me how to hold a match at arm's length and turn the burner on with the other hand.

She got her first Maytag wringer washing machine, and it occupied a spot in the corner of the porch. No water was piped into the house, so she ran a hose from a hydrant in the yard next door. She complained about using cold water, but with good washing powder, the clothes came out clean. When we finished the laundry, we lugged the tubs of water through the kitchen, out the back door, and across the yard. The vacant lot was a perfect place to dump dirty water because the sand soaked it up.

∿

Next to Whitley Avenue, Dairy Avenue was the busiest street in town. Devaney's Grocery Store was a quarter of a mile down from our house. Beyond that was a tavern and another labor camp where Mexican workers lived. When Daddy wasn't home, Tink and I liked to sit on the steps and watch traffic and wave at anyone we knew who passed by. If Daddy caught us, he'd say, "You girls get in the house. It don't look good for you to set out here."

Next to us, a big house sat on cement blocks, and behind it, next to our backyard, there were rows of one-room cabins. Whole families lived in each one. The rustic cabins surrounded a shower house and a line of six smelly toilets. Occasionally someone filled the toilet holes with bags of lime.

Late one evening, I got down on my hands and knees and looked under the house. I could see people milling around over at the camp. Barefoot kids were chasing one another. I saw a young mother in a faded dress, carrying a baby on her hip, enter the community shower.

A car loaded with field hands pulled into the camp and parked between two cabins. As the workers unloaded, I counted eight people. A very tired-looking old woman, her cotton sack draped across her shoulder, trudged across the dirty lot toward the toilet. Later, we got to know and love Maw Proctor and her family. They had come from Alabama and, like us, they were there to put down roots. They are one of the few families that still remain in Corcoran, like the Grants.

Daddy was always warning us to stay out of the camp, so when I heard him pull into the yard I hurried to the back door. Mama dropped her sack on the porch and drew a deep sigh as if it was an effort just to walk through the door. She acted too tired to eat. She held Jimmy in her lap and fed him from her plate. With tears in her eyes, she said, "He cries ever' mornin' when I leave him."

Daddy reached around her and patted her shoulder. "We ain't stayin' here, Mama. Soon as we get enough money together, we're goin' back home. We ain't never worked this hard before. You and me both work sun up to sun down in this awful heat. I don't see how we could buy school lunches for six kids right now if they didn't work on Saturdays."

"But maybe one of these days you can get a job drivin' a tractor. That ain't as hard, not like pickin' cotton, and it pays more."

"I don't know, Mama. I just can't see much hope."

I wondered who was right. I was homesick, but I was making a few friends. Mama kept saying we would find a better house. With some of the money I had earned, I bought new clothes. I still missed Tiawah High School and my friends. I was beginning to feel torn.

Kitty climbed up on the bench beside Mama and picked up Jimmy's baby-soft hand and kissed it. Mama looked down at her and smiled.

With nine kids, still it was quiet at the table. I forgot my spying at the camp. As Tink and I cleaned up the kitchen, all I could think about was Daddy's talk of leaving. I knew Mama had hopes of things getting better, and I tried to imagine how that could happen. I missed Oklahoma, but part of me wanted to stay and make life better where I was.

One day Daddy met a man in the field from Roswell, New Mexico. He came with his family every fall to work the cotton season, then they returned to Roswell. I heard him tell Daddy that the big farmers in California owned almost all the land, that a little guy didn't stand a chance. "But there's a lot of little farms in New Mexico, especially around Roswell." That was all Daddy needed to hear.

Now it was, "As soon as we can get enough money together, we'll see if we can find a little farm for rent near Roswell."

When Aunt Ida heard about this talk, she was upset. Almost every evening I watched her walk across the open field in back of our house. I can still see her lift the barbwire fence and crawl under. She had to wade through deep sand, then stop at the edge of our yard and empty her shoes. She said things like, "Bill, I don't understand why you talk like that. You ain't got no family in either place, Oklahoma or New Mexico. Addie and me lived for the day when you and your family would come. It'd break our hearts now to see you leave.

You're a hard worker and dependable. The farmers like that. You don't have to pick cotton forever. You can drive a tractor or irrigate. You can get a job at the cotton gin. Things will get better in the spring. You'll see."

"Idie," Daddy said, "it takes the whole family to make a decent wage here. How am I ever gonna make a livin' without Elsie workin' like a slave? We got babies that need her. She ain't never left our babies with someone else."

Back and forth they went, Aunt Ida promising things would improve, and Daddy worrying they wouldn't. In a while they would talk about the hard times they had had in the past, how their parents had died too young, and Daddy ended up confessing he had been through much worse.

❧

I think leaving Oklahoma was like a death to my daddy. It would take two long years for him to work through his grief, and for his small-farm dreams to fade. As for me, I was at the vulnerable age of fifteen. Long after the pain of that drastic move ceased, the memories lingered on. They still do.

Christmas

THE SUN SHONE all the month of December, even on Christmas Day. The brisk cool air of early morning didn't last long. By the end of the school day, as Tink and I walked the five blocks toward home, then cut across a field through tall dead weeds, the sun grew hotter by the minute. We came upon barefoot children escaping the sun in the shade of the cabins, and I couldn't help wondering if my old Oklahoma friends were wading in snow.

At home, Tink and I changed into work clothes and waited for Sid and the twins. When Daddy and Mama came home, we were all ready to return with him to the field, where we picked cotton until dusk.

One Saturday afternoon, we cashed our cotton tickets and went to town. Tink and I crossed the field to Aunt Ida's, and then Louise walked with us the remaining ten blocks to town. Men and women from the fields crowded the sidewalk all along the main block of the business district. Men gathered on the street corners while women shopped at the Mercantile, J.C. Penney Co., and the Coronet five and dime store. I hurried to the post office where my heart leaped as I worked the combination to Box 125 and pulled out a letter from my friend Lola. I tucked it in my pocket, saving it until I got home.

It was early December, and silver ropes already crisscrossed the tops of intersections, with a big red bell hanging in the center of each. In the middle of town stood a tall tree wrapped in silver tinsel with red and green bulbs. Stores had painted their windows with manger scenes, holly, Christmas trees, and Santa Claus figures. When we stepped inside, we were greeted with familiar carols. Aunt Ida laughed when I said it felt like Christmas in July. We had to almost run to keep up with her as she hurried into J.C. Penney and straight to the yardage department.

Along the wall were fabrics in both solid and gingham checks of many colors, and a little farther on, there was a table of prints. I spotted a bolt of red roses and thought of Mama.

We waited with Aunt Ida while the fabric clerk, Hester Thigpin, measured, cut, and folded the materials Aunt Ida had chosen and recorded the amounts on a small pad. She said, "How do you find time to sew? Aren't you pickin' cotton now?" Aunt Ida put her money on the counter and said, "I'm lookin' ahead to winter. I'll catch up on my sewin' while there ain't no work in the fields."

"Smart thinkin'," Hester said. She reached up for a metal container and unscrewed it, leaving the lid attached to a cable. She continued to talk to Aunt Ida while she put money and the receipt into the metal cup. She screwed the lid back on and pulled hard on a cord. The money in the cup then crossed the store above our heads, traveling up the cable to a cashier sitting behind a desk upstairs who made change and sent it back down.

At home, I opened Lola's letter in the privacy of my bedroom. She had sent me one of her school pictures. She had written about the basketball games. I closed my eyes and tried to imagine myself there among my friends, chasing the ball and passing it off to Esther. Or maybe sitting in the bleachers, watching Bill travel up and down the polished floor of that beautiful old hardwood court. A deep depression settled over me. I was homesick, with little relief in sight.

か

The Saturday before Christmas, Mama sent Tink and me with Daddy to Hanford to buy new shoes for Christmas. We drove past the turnoff to the fields and traveled north for eighteen miles, past farmhouses and wide-open spaces where crops had already been plowed under. When an old schoolhouse came into view in the distance, Daddy said, "Addie and Ivan used to live out here somewhere. That's where their kids went to grade school." He said the school was closed now.

Near Hanford, we passed an old cemetery, then crossed the railroad tracks and drove down main street. The town was larger than Corcoran, but it was decorated in much the same style. We admired a Christmas tree in one of the store windows and then went into the shoe store where there were many shoes showcased. Tink and I each got new brown-and-white saddle oxfords. It was the first of many visits to a place everyone called "The Jew Store." Operated by a Jewish couple and their daughter, it was one of a chain of shoe stores, Kirby's. In the sixties, I realized what a bigoted reference our casual title for the store was.

During the Christmas school break, I watched the kids from the labor camp congregate in our backyard to play jump rope and hopscotch in the dirt in their bare feet. My younger brother and sisters played, too, of course, but I couldn't help comparing their fun with my own young life in Oklahoma. I had had many more activities on rich, beautiful land, many more ways to challenge my growing body and to expose myself to the world's wonders. My siblings' lives were so small here in this camp. I thought, "My God, what have we done? If we stay here, they will be robbed of their childhood." And sadness overtook me as I realized that the innocence and simplicity of my own childhood was fast slipping away.

On Christmas Eve I went to town with Daddy and the kids. He held two-year-old Kitty in his arms as we waited in a long line of fidgety kids for a chance to see Santa Claus. Santa stood at the foot of a brightly lit Christmas tree, handing out bags of candy and apples and oranges. When Kitty's turn came, Santa said, "Merry Christmas, blue eyes!"

On the way home, Daddy dropped me off at the Assembly of God Church. I hurried to join my cousin Loraine and a group of other young people boarding a Sunday school bus. We pulled away and Florence Hampton began playing her accordion. We sang Christmas carols as we rode up and down the quiet streets.

We made one important stop, in front of Esther Hammond's home. Her father, Reverend Brother Eyer, had built the church when Esther was a young woman. She was now married to a prominent Corcoran businessman. We got out and sang carols under her big double window. Inside, a spotlight shone behind a silver tree decorated with lights and bulbs and bows. When we finished "Silent Night," Esther opened the door, waved to us, and handed a plate of cookies out the door. As we got back on the bus, crying out "Merry Christmas! Merry Christmas!," there was a touch of holiday spirit in the air.

With January, enough rain finally came to settle the dust. After that, a cold gray fog hovered over the valley and I could hardly believe that Christmas had come and gone.

Faith

MY ASSOCIATION WITH THE YOUTH GROUP at the Assembly of God Church was interrupted when Aunt Ida told Daddy about a young Indian man who was holding a revival meeting at her church. "He plays a guitar and sings, and there's a boy that plays a banjo. The two of them harmonize, and it's about the prettiest singin' I ever heard."

That night, Daddy took Tink and me to check it out. The house was packed with people from the fields. We sat near the back, clapping our hands and singing the old familiar hymns along with the rest of the crowd. At the front of the church, a choir swayed back and forth as they clapped to the rhythm of the music. A tall dark young man with a mass of coal black hair stood in the front row, strumming a guitar. A toddler wearing a frilly red dress came up the aisle to the front of the congregation and the young preacher smiled, obviously proud as his pretty wife picked the child up.

Next to the man, a teenage boy was seated. His left hand moved quickly along the frets on the neck of a banjo, while his right hand beat out an Appalachian sound that rose above the noise of the crowd.

The pastor stepped in front of the podium and motioned to the congregation with both hands. Everyone rose, and as they became more emotional, they waved their arms above their heads, and their bodies swayed back and forth in time to the music. Clapping hands was nothing new to Tink and me, but we had never seen anything like this.

A few benches ahead of us a chunky little woman threw her hands in the air and leaped into the aisle. She shouted *hallelujah*s and danced up and down. Her eyes were shut tight, and I thought she would fall as she bumped into people, but when she touched someone, she just bounced away and never missed a beat. The walls vibrated with *hallelujah*s and *amen*s, and I looked over at Daddy. He was clapping his hands lightly, tears streaming down his face. He was smiling.

When the crowd finally settled down, the young Indian guitar-playing evangelist stepped to the podium, accompanied by his friend the banjo player. The crowd sat, spellbound, as they played and sang. I was sure Daddy was enjoying them, but it made me sad that his tears kept rolling.

I don't remember anything about the sermon that night. I remember a crowded altar and a service that was still going strong when Daddy leaned over to Tink and me and said, "Let's go home. Mama and me gotta work tomorrow and you girls got school." In the truck, he said he thought the preachers ought to remember the congregation was made up of hardworking folks.

We attended the revival almost every night for two weeks. I listened to the music and dreamed of owning a guitar. Daddy must have been impressed by the music, too, because, careful as he was with money, he came home one day with a black guitar case. Of course when he placed it on the table, it was Robert he called to see it. I caught my breath when he lifted the lid to reveal a nearly new Harmony guitar. Daddy had bought it cheap from a man in the field. He thought Robert might want to learn to play, but Robert had a girlfriend, and he never showed much interest in the guitar.

I found an instruction book in the bottom of the case and looked it over for a few days. Then I taught myself a few chords. I had some kind of mental block, though. I simply couldn't hear the changes. I followed the book and strummed until I could play Stephen C. Foster's "Old Black Joe." I played it for months, until I could make the changes smoothly. Then one day, after a year, click! I heard the changes in my head and I shoved the instruction book aside. I was playing the guitar.

After that I joined others from the field who congregated at the church on the corner of Chittenden and Bainum. Our friends knew gospel and folk music and encouraged me to bring my guitar to church. They helped me keep it in tune. I sat with them on the platform and strummed to every song, knowing that if I made a mistake, no one would hear it above the noise of the congregation.

Then the church got a new pastor. Brother Jefferson liked to jump and yell and put on a show. Daddy called it "playing church." Church attendance dropped to almost nothing. One night Brother Jefferson jumped up on top of a bench and ran from it to another to another all the way to the back of the church. Then he hit the floor, staggered, and caught the wall. I thought he would break his neck. Daddy was so mad he growled all the way home. After we went to bed, I could hear him raving to Mama about "all that foolishness."

What puzzled me was why Daddy stayed with the church. Now I'm sure it was because he felt at home. Church was important to him. He wanted to be among the poor, hardworking people like himself. For me, Brother Jefferson was an addition to the nightmare of the time. I found peace among the chords of my Harmony guitar.

The headaches Daddy suffered in Oklahoma only seemed to get worse and more frequent after we moved. When he was offered a job baling hay at night, he hesitated, knowing it could be bad for him to breathe the dust and chaff. Bucking hay was one of the most strenuous jobs a farm worker could do. Daddy was well aware of that, but the pay was good and he thought he would bring home more money.

The first morning that he came home after working all night in the hay field, he was covered with chaff from head to toe. He dropped his lunch box on the floor just inside the door and stopped to wash up using a tub beside the washing machine.

As I looked across the breakfast table at his bloodshot eyes, I couldn't remember ever seeing him so tired. He could hardly hold his eyes open. When he placed his hot coffee cup against the side of his face, I knew he had a headache, and I knew what that meant.

When Daddy had a headache, it sometimes lasted for several days. He couldn't stand noise. Mama put hot towels on his head to ease the pain. Aspirin did no good at all.

I was always reminded of the fact that his mother, who had died young, had had headaches, too. I grew up knowing this, and my young mind had been convinced that Daddy would die young like she did. I wanted to put my arms around him and tell him how much I loved him and would like to take away his pain. But I knew I couldn't do that. I was too big.

Susie, who had just turned six a few days earlier, stood up on the bench and worked her way down the wall behind June and Judy. Daddy smiled down at her as she stood beside him while he ate his breakfast. It had become a ritual for Susie, especially when he wasn't feeling good or was late getting home from work.

Mama looked at him and said, "You got a headache, don't you, Daddy?"

"Yeah. I don't know how long I can do this. I sure understand why they work nights. It'd be almost impossible in the heat of the day. Even at night, the chaff blows and gets down inside your clothes. It sticks to your sweaty skin and itches somethin' awful. It fills the air and makes it hard to breathe. I gotta get me one of them respirators to wear over my mouth and nose before I go back."

"Don't go back tonight, Daddy. Drive over and tell the boss you can't work nights. It ain't worth it."

"I can't quit just like that. They have a hard time gettin' hands at night. Mr. Sheffield helped me get this job and I can't quit right now. I'll try it a while longer."

Daddy worked nights for about six weeks. But he was never really able to make more money in the hay fields. Sometimes the wind blew all night and they couldn't work. He had trouble sleeping days, and his headaches got worse.

Mama put a spoonful of Vicks salve in a quart jar and filled it with hot water. She made a tent with a towel, and Daddy breathed the vapor.

The kids played outside, and we all knew not to make noise at the table. It was amazing how the little kids knew. I often saw them staring at him sadly as he sat with one elbow on the table and the side of his head resting in the palm of his left hand while he ate very slowly with his right. I wondered what was going through their minds. I was so sure we would lose him. It never occurred to me at the time, but they were probably afraid of losing him, too.

Uncle Ivan told Daddy about a Chinese doctor in Hanford who treated headaches. Daddy drove over there and came home with a big bag of smelly herbs. Mama boiled some of them and a terrible medicinal odor filled the air. She made a tea from the herbs and Daddy drank it, but I don't remember if it helped him. I do know he still had the headaches off and on for several more years. Then another evangelist came to town for a one-week revival meeting at the Assembly of God Church.

One evening there was a special service for the anointing of the sick. Daddy had been anointed before, many times, and he got in line with the others, as always. He made his way to the front of the church as Tink and I sat in the back and watched. When the service was over, we went home and nothing was said.

Then, one evening at supper several months later, Mama said, "Daddy, I'm almost afraid to say this, but you ain't had a headache lately."

Daddy sat quietly, staring at the table. Tears came to his eyes and his voice quivered as he tried to speak. "The last night that young evangelist was here, I was anointed. He said to me, 'You won't have this kind of headache no more.' And I felt it too. I mean I really felt that my headaches was gone. For weeks I thought my head itched inside. I don't know. I can't say no more. I'm afraid to talk about it. Afraid I'll lose it."

I must say, I don't know, either. I only know that Daddy's headaches were a part of my childhood, and to my knowledge, after that last anointing, he never had another one. He was always reluctant to talk about it.

My theory is that Daddy had migraines or terrible tension headaches, probably increased by his enormous responsibilities. Sometimes things came crashing down on him. The headaches were the way his body reacted to the stress.

Then one day his faith somehow helped him put it down.

Memorial Day

THE WINTER WAS HARD. I remember my birthday, February 10, 1948, as cold and foggy. Cotton season was over and migrant workers had moved on to pick oranges. As tractors plowed stalks under in the lake basin, we pulled bolls for Mr. Kirkendal, a small farmer in the community of Waukena. The field had been picked, and scattered bolls left on the stalks were cracked open, exposing cotton inside. After a cold five-mile ride in the back of the pickup, we walked through wet foliage and found a few rows with bolls clinging to the stalks. I pulled on my well-worn cotton gloves and began snapping off handfuls of the bolls and stuffing them into my sack.

Fog settled like a mist over the field. The damp penetrated my chambray work shirt. Soon my gloves were damp and the sharp empty burrs on the stalks picked at my fingers through the wet gloves, and the tips of my fingers felt like ice. By noon, a cold drizzle drove us from the field. At the scales, I heard Mr. Kirkendal say, "Well, that's it. I might as well plow it under now. Ain't enough left to mess with." On the way home, Robert and Susie rode in the front with Daddy, while the rest of us huddled against the cab in the bed of the pickup. The warm, old house on Dairy Avenue was a welcome refuge after the shivering ride through the fog and rain.

Then came the March winds that swept across the dry fields, kicking up clouds of dust. They rolled across Dairy Avenue and through our yard. Mama stood in the living room window and watched the dust blow. Every day, she waited for Daddy to drive into the yard after another discouraging day of searching for work. He often commented, "That dust's more blindin' to drive in than the fog."

We lived on savings for two months as Daddy tried in vain to find work. Then one day he walked through the door with a big brown box of food. He set it on the table and pulled out plainly marked containers that read Powdered Eggs and Powdered Milk. He told Mama he had stood in a long line at the Grange Hall to get the groceries.

Mama said, "I'd never heard of such things."

Daddy laughed. "I never did either. We always milked the cows and gathered the eggs, didn't we? I wish we had the cows and chickens back, but we don't." He handed one of the boxes to Mama and said, "Let's give it a try."

Soon Mama had a pitcher filled with milk. She poured out a glass of it and we all sampled it. Daddy said, "It ain't fresh cow's milk, but it tastes like milk, don't it?"

I thought it tasted strong, but I didn't say. I learned to water it down to take away the strange taste.

The next morning, Mama added some of that milk to the powdered eggs, along with salt and pepper, and cooked them in a skillet. They were the best scrambled eggs I had ever tasted. As we sat around finishing our breakfast, Aunt Ida walked in the back door. The plainly marked packages sat on the cabinet. Mama said, "I meant to put that stuff away."

Daddy said, "Ida won't tell nobody."

Aunt Ida said, "I won't say anything if you don't want me to. But I came because I was worried you might be gettin' low on money. And I wanted to tell you Addie and me got commodities lots of times."

"I don't want the relatives talkin'," Daddy said.

"Truth be known, Bill," she said, "probably every one of the relatives had to do the same thing at one time or other." She laughed and made Mama and Daddy laugh.

Later Mama and I talked about the commodities food some more. Mama said she thought things would get better, but Daddy was discouraged.

Finally, in April, work opened up. Daddy learned to drive a tractor for the first time as he plowed the ground to make ready for a new cotton crop.

As the days grew warm, Mama planted morning glory seeds outside the living room window. "To block the hot afternoon sun," she said. By the time we moved from Dairy Avenue, the vine, with its pale blue blossoms, decorated the area around the window, climbed around the corner onto the porch, and shaded the front of the house.

By the time school was over, the fields were green with tiny cotton stalks ready to be thinned. Daddy was plowing somewhere in the lake basin. Mama, Sid, and I rode out Whitley Avenue with Aunt Addie in the cool early morning hours of Memorial Day. Our thirteen-year-old cousin Earl was with us.

Aunt Addie's driving kept us all laughing as we crept along in the two-door Chevy sedan. She was only four feet, eleven inches tall, and though she sat on a cushion, she still could barely see over the steering wheel. When she braked and pushed in on the clutch, she had to stretch her short legs as far as she could and push with her stubby toes to reach the pedals. The car always jumped when she let out the clutch. Oncoming drivers often did a doubletake as they passed, seeing what must have looked like a wig behind the steering wheel. Earl curled up on the floor in the back, pretending he had to hide until we were out of town.

We stopped on the edge of a field where Uncle Ivan was hard at work unloading an armful of old hoes from the back of a pickup. It was six o'clock in the morning and already he was sweating as he sharpened hoes with a hand file.

Turning to Mama, he said, "Elsie, if I remember right, you can put a sharp edge on a hoe." He handed her a new file and she picked up a hoe from the top of the pile. She got on her knees on the ground, placed the file on the edge of the blade, and slid it up and down, making a dull screeching sound. She handed that sharp hoe to Sid and told him to give it to me and get another hoe from the pile. She worked with Uncle Ivan and a couple of other men until all the hoes were ready to go.

Uncle Ivan's crew, one of many in the lake basin, consisted of around thirty women and children taking advantage of the long weekend break from school. There were also a few white men and a dozen or so Mexicans.

Before assigning rows, Uncle Ivan gave us a lesson on how to thin our first row of cotton. He borrowed my short, rough-handled hoe. When he took it, it caused a splinter in my hand. He handed it back and reached for another.

In Oklahoma, we had weeded our small patches of cotton carefully so that we didn't cut down the scarce stalks. The long rows in the lake basin were a solid green line with few spaces between thick, healthy stalks. Uncle Ivan told us that we should leave a space no more than three stalks, about the width of our hoe handle, apart. He chopped out a space to demonstrate for us. Sid took his shoes off and tossed them down at the end of the row, and we started down a mile-long row into the heat of that first summer.

No one had prepared us for that first day. In thirty minutes, I was thirsty. There was a long aluminum tank of water set on a wooden wagon in the middle of the field. We had to thin a row for half a mile before we got to it and could get a drink of water.

By the time we reached the wagon, I was desperate for a drink. A dozen or so tin cans were on the wagon beside the tank. A few lay in the dirt. When we neared the wagon, I dropped my hoe and ran. I handed Mama an empty can, grabbed one for myself, and got in line. There were three or four people in line ahead of us, and I felt my parched lips reach for every drop of water that fell from their cans as they drank.

Mama said, "I never felt such thirst. I didn't dream it'd be like this."

I filled my can with water and changed cups with her as Sid got a drink. I filled another can for me and stepped aside to drink.

Mama was wearing an old bonnet she had brought from Oklahoma. I was bareheaded, wearing a skirt and short-sleeved blouse. As we returned to our rows, Sid pulled his shirt off and tied it around his waist. Mama told him to put it back on, because he would burn. Then she turned to me and said, "You need something on your head and arms."

The day grew hotter and hotter. Sid's feet burned as he tried to walk in the blistering sand. The clods hurt his feet. Mama dug through the topsoil to find cool earth where he could put his feet while we thinned his row for him. It slowed us so that we were even longer getting to the water wagon the second time. The thirst was torture. The water was warm. Sid crawled under the wagon in the shade, and Mama cried.

Back at our rows, I happened to look toward the end of the field at our cars and saw that they were sitting in a pool of water. I told Sid, "Look! The irrigation water is gettin' away. We won't be able to get the car out."

Sid was excited. "Maybe we can go swimmin' when we stop to eat."

I called to Earl to look at the cars sitting in water. He laughed and laughed, and soon everybody near us was laughing, too. He said, "Haven't you ever seen a mirage before?"

"What's a mirage?"

"It's caused from the heat." He kept laughing while he tried to convince me the cars were OK. When we drew nearer the vehicles, the pool of water backed off and the atmosphere around it was murky and fluttery. No, I had never seen a mirage.

Mama called to me. "Betty, run to the car and get Sid's shoes." Sid yelled, "I throwed 'em on the ground at the end of our first row."

Walking back between the rows, my head throbbed as the sun beat on the top of my skull.

The sand had burned the bottom of Sid's feet bright red. His face twisted with pain as he forced his feet into his shoes. Leaving them untied, he hobbled along until we reached the end of our rows.

When we stopped for lunch, my arms were glowing pink and the sun burned me even more. Mosquitos from the irrigation ditch a few yards away bothered me, and when I slapped at them, my skin stung with pain. My head was throbbing in the hundred-degree heat, my face was beet red, and my legs ached.

Uncle Ivan had cold water in the back of his pickup. He tipped the jug and I could hear chunks of ice rattling. I was hungry but too tired to eat. I just wanted to lie in the shade of the car with my eyes closed.

There were no toilets in the fields. I tried to hide from the rest of the crew behind Aunt Addie's car. Mama opened the front door to make a shield. Then my monthly cycle took me by surprise. Mama said, "If only we had a way home, but Addie's already back out there in the heat. She must be used to it." She took a faded bandana from her pocket, folded it, and handed it to me. I prepared myself as best I could for the long afternoon.

Mama told me to lie down in the car and rest, but I couldn't rest, knowing we would soon go back to work. By the end of the day, working in heat that soared to 100 degrees, my face and arms were badly burned. To make things worse, a truck came and took the water wagon to the far end of the field, making our row a mile long before we could get a drink. When Mama asked Uncle Ivan why they moved the water, he said the foreman said the Mexican men were standing around the wagon too long. I had never encountered that kind of prejudice. I thought it was the cruelest act I had ever seen. Why would one person deny another a drink of water, especially in that kind of heat?

Tink had supper ready when we got home. I fell across the bed too sick and tired to eat. I couldn't bear to be touched. Mama brought me a couple of aspirin and insisted I come to the table and eat a few bites.

The next morning, I was unable to go to school. I was sick for three days. On Friday I went in to pick up my grades and clean out my locker.

We thinned and weeded cotton all summer. I wore a long-sleeved, blue chambray work shirt. Mama made me a bonnet. Later, I paid $1.98 for a big sombrero to shade my face. The hat allowed a bit of breeze to hit my face. My worst memory of the work is the awful thirst.

Weeding Fields

FOR TWO SUMMERS, Mama and I worked on a crew that thinned a square-mile section in the lake basin called the Progressive Ranch. The row boss was called Arkie, and he worked for a foreman named Fred White, who worked for Salyer Land Company. Arkie was the best row boss we ever had.

One morning Arkie caught sight of me lagging behind Mama. Mama had been helping me catch up. I had suffered my first big heartache over a boy who had married someone else. Arkie walked across the field with a bucket of water. He heard Mama scolding me. As I was lifting the dipper to my lips, I heard him say, "Mrs. Grant, leave Betty alone. She's a hard worker."

"She daydreams too much," Mama said.

"I ain't never seen her standin' around leanin' on her hoe handle," Arkie said. "And there's somethin' else I noticed about Betty. She works steady, and no matter how much you fuss and scold her, she ain't gonna go no faster, 'cause she's only got one gear."

His remark gave the crew a big laugh and caused Mama to let up on me. She kept her eyes peeled, but didn't turn back on my row unless I ran into a bad spot of Bermuda grass and got too far behind. Sometimes Arkie even came to help me catch up.

Our hats, bonnets, and long sleeves protected us from the sun but not from the crop dusting. The small planes swept over us, spraying pesticides from the backends. A grayish white cloud spread out across the field, covering the cotton and the workers, along with any kids who happened to be in the field. The smell reminded me of fly spray. My eyes and nose burned, and I coughed like a habitual smoker.

One morning, our bodies swayed from the draft of a crop duster as it dipped down and then roared overhead. Arkie's hat sailed across the field and I dropped my hoe, grabbed my sombrero, and hung on tight. Mama braced herself and clung to her hoe.

The plane zoomed out of the field and circled for a return run. She looked up and complained, "There ain't no sense in them planes comin' so close. It's dangerous." Then she groaned and covered the side of her face with her hand. A speck of something from the spray had struck just below her eye and burned a tiny hole in her face.

The next weekend, Daddy's boss Bill Dethro came to our door early on Sunday morning to give Daddy instructions about a job the next day. When Daddy came back in the house, he said, "I'm glad you all wasn't out in the field this mornin.' Bill said one of them little planes was tryin' to pull up outta the field and it hit a power line. It crashed and burned. The pilot was killed."

Then he said, "Do you girls know a young man from Tulare that married the oldest Blakely girl?"

"I know who he is," I said. "He used to pick Helen up at school during lunch hours."

"He's the one who got killed this mornin'."

What started out as a normal Sunday changed quickly as word of the accident spread. Sadness fell over the town. But Monday morning, life was back to normal for us. Mama and I returned to Arkie's crew, and in the distance, I could still see small planes dive down, release streams of pesticide, and pull back up just above the power lines. I thought about Daddy farther out in the lake basin riding along on a tractor. He always said we worked harder than he did. He said, "If there's any breeze at all, I feel it up there movin' along through the field. But I get paid more. It don't make sense."

One day the temperature soared to 116 degrees. At noon Arkie called it a day. He said, "A body could die out here." I ran to the water wagon to get myself a drink and splash water on my face. Sitting in the shade of the tank, I listened as others drank their fill and chatted. I couldn't believe we were going home early.

That evening, Daddy cried when Mama told him we had quit early. He said he had worried himself sick all day. "There ain't no such thing as a breeze out there. It's the most penetratin' heat I ever knowed." Then he said, "We're gettin' outta here one a these days, Mama. We're gonna go back home."

⤳

Later that summer, Tink and Sid and I weeded cotton so we could buy school clothes. We were at the field by six o'clock in the morning. The cotton was waist high, and in the early morning hours, it was dripping wet with dew. I waded into the tall foliage with a freshly sharpened hoe. Within minutes, there wasn't a dry thread in my clothes from the waist down. Mama worried that Tink and I would get sick, especially on certain days of the month. Looking back, I chuckle to remember that she didn't allow us to wash our hair during those few days, but we could always keep working.

By midmorning the sun was hot enough to dry the green leaves and our clothes, and by the time we stopped to eat our lunch, the temperature was close to a hundred degrees.

Sometimes we ran into strips of Bermuda grass and spent all afternoon away from the water wagon. The row boss, Mr. Burnes, carried an aluminum bucket of water down the row from person to person until all of us had a drink. His wife weeded cotton with the crew. She was about five feet, two inches tall, very thin and stooped, and I thought of her as a little old lady. She wore a bonnet, but the shriveled skin on her sun-darkened face had deep creases like dried leather. The fields aged people fast. Thinking of the Burneses today, I realize they were probably still in their forties.

We earned seventy-five cents an hour, and Mr. Burnes paid us on Saturday at noon. As soon as we got home, Tink and I cleaned up and headed downtown to pick out material for school clothes. We also put Lana Turner-style sweaters on layaway. By the time we got them out, Mama would have made new skirts to match. Any style we liked, she could copy.

One day I saw a gingham dress in a shop window in Hanford. The low round neck and dropped waist were lined with scallops of the same material, small turquoise and white checks, and around the edges of each scallop was a row of tiny white lace. Mama said, "Honey, I can make you a dress just like that. Let's go to Penneys and see if we can find that material."

J.C. Penney Co. had checked gingham in every imaginable color. Mama picked up a bolt of turquoise and white right away, and then picked up a roll of white lace. A few days later, she cut a pattern and fitted it to me. "Stand up straight," she said, holding the paper to my shoulder. "Now turn around and raise your arm so I can measure armholes and darts."

We had been through the same procedure many times to get a basic fit. She cut the pattern from newspaper, dropped the neck and waist, then trimmed the dress with lace. Before the day was over, I had a dress exactly like the one in the dress shop window.

She sewed for five of us that year, because Susie started first grade.

The clothes helped the way I felt about myself. So did getting a class ring, which would be coming soon. I could feel my homesickness growing lighter, even though I had a hard time making friends. Mostly, I stayed to myself, except for lunch hour, when I could be with Tink and Louise, Okies just like me.

Touched by Love

DADDY ALWAYS TOLD US, "Be proud you're Okies." He used the word with pride, and he loved to tell jokes he picked up in the field. His favorite was about a family of Okies whose car broke down on Route 66. While they were stranded somewhere in the middle of Arizona, they attended a revival meeting. During the altar call, the preacher walked back, took the Oklahoma farmer by the hand, and said, "Mister, wouldn't you like to go to Heaven?"

The man looked at the preacher and answered, "Well, sir, you'll have to talk to my wife. We've started to California."

We laughed at Daddy's jokes, but we knew the word *Okies* was down there with *nigger* and *wetback*. I went from class to class at school, and when the bell rang at day's end, I ran out the door and headed for home and the safety of the old shack on the edge of the labor camp.

On Sunday mornings, I listened to Sister Jefferson read from the Book of Revelations, the only book of the Bible she seemed to know. Her sermons were all gloom and doom. She warned us of war and more war. She said Christians were going to be put to death for their faith. "You better be ready," she said, "'cause we are livin' in the last days. It's gonna take all the faith you can muster up to give your life for the cause of Christ."

Brother Jefferson, on the other hand, preached hellfire, and I thought if what he said was true, I didn't have a chance. I told Tink, "I don't believe anyone knows how to interpret Revelations." I was afraid to say that openly with anyone else. I had seen people dragged to the altar to beg forgiveness, but I knew my words were safe with my sister.

I was two thousand miles from familiar surroundings, where even in the years we had been at war, I felt safe among my family and community. Now I was in a strange place that blazed with heat, or covered me with a dark mist. Still, sometimes I looked up and saw snow-white clouds hovering, and I felt they showered me with love.

One Sunday night, Tink and I came home from church with Daddy to a quiet house. We walked past Robert and Sid sleeping on the front porch. Mama and the baby, Jimmy, were resting quietly on a bed in the living room. I reached for the cord to turn off the light, trying to be quiet, so as not to wake our four younger sisters, who were asleep in wall-to-wall beds.

Nothing was unusual about that night. The room went dark, and we climbed under the covers to settle down to sleep. As I remember, I had just closed my eyes when a small square of light, like a picture frame, appeared in front of my face. At the bottom of the picture, I saw an explosion. A cloud of smoke rose from the ground, boiled up, and formed a mushroom cloud. As fast as it appeared, it was gone. A feeling of ecstasy swept over me, and as I lay awake, an aura of peace surrounded me.

The next morning, I awoke to a world afire with love. As we walked through the labor camp on our way to school, I felt as if I were being lifted off the ground. I walked on a cloud above all the hurt. The sensation stayed with me all day, as I moved from class to class. I was a misfit among a field of strangers.

That evening, Daddy went to the store and bought groceries. He walked into the kitchen when he returned and tossed the Hartford *Sentinel* on the table. My eyes fell on a black-and-white picture that covered almost half of the front page. It was the bomb! The mushroom cloud of smoke. I had been hearing about the atomic bomb for almost three years, but I had never seen a photograph of it. Now there it was, the very same image that had flashed in front of my eyes the night before in the darkness of my bedroom.

On an island far out in the Pacific Ocean, they were testing a bomb much larger than the ones they had dropped on Hiroshima and Nagasaki. This bomb made those two look small.

Yet the ecstatic feeling stayed with me for days. I didn't know what it meant. I didn't know how to think about it, and I didn't ask. It would be more than twenty years before I told the story to anyone.

Friends

WHEN YOU SPEND TIME, month after month, out in the fields with people, you come to know them in a peculiar way. You form a special kind of bond, though you might not even know their last names. But they mean something to you because, like you, they had dreams and they worked hard too. Many of the people who lived in the labor camps were families who had come to put down roots. They saved a portion of their wages in an effort to get out of the camp into something of their own. But not everyone could take the work and the conditions. Some of them drank and fought.

I remember Mama saying, "Seems like some folks work all week and drink all weekend." One week, Grandma and Grandpa came to see us. Sirens blared and I heard Mama say to Grandma, "I swear there ain't a weekend goes by them sirens don't go barrelin' down Dairy Avenue, picking someone up and haulin' them into jail or the hospital or something. You ain't never seen such fightin' and stabbin' and beatin' each other half to death."

"That's what drinkin' does, Elsie," Grandma said. "It changes a person. They say some folks like to drink and laugh and whoop it up, and others, well, they just get downright mean."

Mama said, "Yeah, and then there's them that cry. They drink to drown their sorrow, but they can't get away from it. Not even with a bottle. They're the saddest of all."

"You know what I think, Mommie? When all the fightin's goin' on, sometimes I think it's 'cause they're so poor. No matter how hard some folks work, they're still poor. That's what they're mad about. That's what they're swingin' their fists at. Sometimes I feel like swingin' my fists, too."

☙

Maybe Mama was thinking about Monk, a young man about thirty years old. He was tall and quiet and a good-looking man. I couldn't understand why he drank so much and wasn't married. He and his nephew, Clayton, lived in a one-room cabin in our camp. Clay was about twenty. Unlike his uncle, he was full of mischief. He loved to find a good green cotton boll and sail it across the field, whacking some fellow worker on the shoulder. Then he'd duck down and hide in the tall cotton. We all laughed at him, especially Sid, and Sid liked to give him a dose of his own medicine.

Monk walked by our house every Saturday afternoon, looking handsome in his clean Levis and a freshly ironed work shirt. One day I sat on the front steps as he headed for the bar about a half mile down the road. He took a fresh pack of cigarettes from his shirt pocket, pulled a piece of cellophane from around the top, and popped the pack against his hand, jarring a couple of cigarettes out the end. A few yards from me he lit up and blew smoke into the air, glancing at me as he passed. But when our eyes met, he ducked his head and kept on going.

A few hours later, he came staggering back. I watched him reeling toward the blacktop, sure he'd fall onto the road and get hit by a car, but each time he faltered, he recovered his balance. It was sad to see him like that.

One day I asked Mama about him and she told me he had been married, but his wife had died giving birth, and the baby had died too. That was when he had started drinking.

"But I never see him drunk during the week," I said. "He works hard and don't talk to anyone. And once in a while, Clay makes him laugh."

"Did you see him passin' just now? Daddy likes him and understands his drinkin', but he'd have a fit if he saw you lookin' at him. You know how Daddy feels."

It was true, Daddy was always trying to protect his six girls. In the field sometimes, I almost died of embarrassment when somebody cussed or said something a little off-color, and Daddy stood up straight and tall and said, "Hey, over there, watch your language! There's women and kids in the field."

I told Mama, "Monk's good-looking when he ain't drunk."

"Yes, he is, but he's a alcoholic. Don't you ever let Daddy see you noticin' him."

I knew she was right, and I knew Monk wasn't gonna talk to me. But I had mixed feelings about him. When I looked at him in the field, I thought he was about the best-looking young man around. But when he caught me looking at him, he always turned away real fast, so I admired him from afar. I just knew he wasn't a bad person, and I wanted to talk to him. Something about him scared me when he was coming home from a bar. He was like a different person. Then when work ended that year, he and his nephew went back to their home in Arkansas and we never saw them again.

❧

One of the most memorable characters we met in the field was Lawrence, an old worker who was over six feet tall and close to three hundred pounds. Because he was so big, he had a hard time getting a ride to work. People just didn't have enough room. I can still see him trudging along clumsily through the field with a heavy load across his shoulder. One day as he reached for a handful of cotton, I noticed his rough hands were scarred and bleeding. I wondered why he didn't get some thin cotton-knit gloves like Mama got for us. All the grocery stores carried them. Mama cut the tips out so we could pick better, and our cuticles took a beating, but the gloves still protected our hands.

Lawrence had scaly patches on his face, and some of the patches were raw. He covered them with something powdery that looked like cornstarch. When I asked Mama what she thought it was, she said the spots were skin cancer caused from all the years he had worked out in the sun.

"Cancer kills people, don't it?" I said.

She said she didn't think skin cancer would killed anyone, but she didn't know if you could heal it, either.

Every time I watched him struggle to get a sack of cotton to the scales, I thought sure he'd fall, but he always made it. Finally I asked Daddy why somebody didn't help him.

Daddy said, "He never fills his sack too full. He goes to the scales with forty or fifty pounds. He knows he can't manage more. He's gettin' old, and he does have to have help emptyin' his sack. If he tried to climb the ladder, he'd fall for sure."

Late one evening, Lawrence headed down through the field, dragging his feet as he followed our rows. Daddy was on one knee, bent across the row gathering cotton from the other side. Lawrence had almost reached Daddy when he stood up with both hands full of fluffy white cotton.

"How you doin', Lawrence?" Daddy said. "Got your five hundred pounds yet?"

Lawrence laughed his usual deep nervous laugh and said, "Why shucks, Mr. Grant, I had that before noon."

We all laughed as Daddy teased. "You're workin' overtime, man. I always go home when I get my five hundred." Lawrence laughed until his big body shook. Daddy had never picked five hundred pounds in one day.

After Lawrence settled down again, he looked at the ground a few seconds and shuffled his feet in the dirt. "Uh, Mr. Grant, I was wonderin' if you folks could give me a ride home this evenin'."

Daddy said there was plenty of room in his pickup. Lawrence's voice trembled as he said thanks.

We weighed up at day's end and threw our empty sacks in the truck bed. Mama climbed into the cab, and Susie ran and took a seat on her lap. Judy opened the door on the driver's side and slid in under the steering wheel and into the middle of the seat. June was right behind her, nudging her way in to make room as Judy slid forward with both hands on the dash.

Before Daddy turned the key in the ignition, he looked back over his shoulder. Tink, Sid, and I were against the cab and Lawrence was at the end of the pickup with his feet dangling.

Daddy called out, "Lawrence, you better climb a little further into the pickup. These levees are bumpy. Wouldn't want you to fall out and get hurt." Lawrence reached back with one arm and got a firm grip on the sideboard, pulling his heavy frame farther into the bed of the truck. He slid his body around, resting his back against the sideboard with both feet out in front of him. He looked uncomfortable but a lot safer.

He lived in a one-room cabin in back of his sister's house. When we reached his home, he wiggled his way off the truck bed and reached for his sack. Sid handed him his beat-up black metal lunch box with an empty thermos rattling around inside. Hanging onto the side of the truck, Lawrence made his way down to where Daddy was. He hesitated for a few seconds, and then he said, "Mr. Grant, I was wonderin' if you could give me a ride to work for a while. I'll give you a quarter a day. I always pay for my rides. Helps buy gas, you know. You just say what time. I won't keep you waitin'."

"You betcha, Lawrence," Daddy said. "Pick you up about six-thirty Monday morning."

So Lawrence rode to work and back with Mama and Daddy for a couple of years. After Daddy started driving a mechanical picker,

Mama had to find another way to work herself. Usually, she rode with Aunt Ida and a group of women. She came home and told us about the people who had given Lawrence a bad time when they had to help him empty a sack, or who had crowded in front of him so that he had to wait in line too long with a heavy load on his shoulder.

Then one evening I walked with Daddy to the grocery store. It was in early September. I heard a familiar laugh and I turned to see Daddy and Lawrence teasing one another. Lawrence said, "Must be nice, ridin' along on one of them picker rigs."

Daddy said, "It's a lot easier on the back, I can tell you that. Who you pickin' for this year? Hand pickin's gettin' kinda scarce, ain't it?"

"I ain't gonna have to worry about it no more. This is my last year to pull a cotton sack. I'll be sixty-five pretty soon. Already signed up for that rockin' chair money."

"You mean next summer when I'm ridin' along in the heat, you gonna be settin' in the shade drinkin' lemonade?"

They both laughed, and Daddy reached out to shake Lawrence's hand. He pulled him forward and embraced him. "Yes, sir," Daddy said, "that's mighty good news."

Three months later, on a cold foggy evening in December, Daddy came home around nine after driving a mechanical picker all day. We had already eaten and cleaned up the kitchen. Mama put Daddy's supper on the table and sat down beside him. "Are you tired, Daddy? You're awful quiet. It must be cold out there after the sun goes down."

"It gets colder every day. Not like that ice and snow in Oklahoma though. I never worked such long hours there, but we're better off here, Mama. There's lots a work for me here." Then Daddy got a lump in his throat. He rested his elbow on the table, put one hand over his eyes, and choked up.

"Why Daddy, what's the matter?" Mama said. It worried her to see Daddy so low. She started talking about how well we were all doing, how we had money in the bank. "You're right. We are better off here," she said.

Daddy wiped his eyes and smiled at her. He knew she had been waiting for him to say those words. But his tears weren't about that. He said, "Mama, Lawrence died this morning."

"Oh my," she said, "Not in the field. He didn't die out there in the cold, did he?"

"He'd been ridin' to work with Slim Porter. He walked out to Dairy Avenue three blocks. When the guys stopped to pick him up, he was settin' on the ground with his back restin' against a power pole. He was wrapped up in his cotton sack to keep warm. Slim called to him, but he didn't answer. They thought he was asleep. One of the guys jumped out of the pickup and ran over to wake him up, but he was dead."

Lawrence had died of a heart attack just a few weeks short of his sixty-fifth birthday. He was gone from our lives. Now I'm saying we didn't forget him.

A Burglary

THE WATTSES MOVED NEXT DOOR to us during our second winter on Dairy Avenue. They were a middle-aged couple. He worked at the Boswell gin and she worked in the fields.

One day, Mrs. Watts knocked at the back door and asked Mama if she would like to have a couple pairs of lace curtains. They'd been worn some, but she didn't need them. The two women hung the curtains and talked as if they'd known each other forever. Mrs. Watts admired Mama's morning glories, wondering how she'd managed to grow them in sand.

Mama said, "I throwed some seed in the ground, watered them a little, and they just took off. Would you like some seed?"

Mrs. Watts laughed and said, "Do you reckon I could make them grow like that?"

Mama shared her morning glories, and from that day on the two of them were friends.

Every morning I watched Mrs. Watts waiting for her ride to work. She sat on a wooden bench inside the screen porch until the faded old green labor bus came into sight. Then she flung the door open and dashed across the street with her lunch pail in one hand and a cotton sack rolled up and tucked under the other arm.

When the weather was warm, the windows of the bus were all rolled down. All the other workers were black, and the workers smiled and called out things like, "Mornin', Dessie, it's gonna be a hot one today." Mrs. Watts climbed onto the bus, where a seat waited for her. She was the one white woman on that rickety old vehicle as it headed toward the lake basin.

Month after month, through thinning, weeding, and picking, she worked with her black friends. People gossiped about her and called her a "nigger lover." I'm sure she knew that, but she never let on; she just kept working. The black contractor got a lot of work for his people, and I never saw her work for anyone else.

Daddy said he wouldn't want Mama working in an all-black crew, because people would talk about her, too. Mama said she didn't see anything wrong with it, but on the other hand, she didn't understand why anyone would want to work in an all-black crew when there was plenty of work elsewhere. She said Mrs. Watts didn't have to subject herself to all that gossip.

It wasn't until after the civil rights movement got underway that I thought seriously about Mrs. Watts and the way she lived her life. She was simply ahead of her time and everyone was too blind to see.

જી

One night there was a loud knock at the back door. It was Mr. Watts calling for Daddy. "Help! Someone's broke into our house!"

I heard Daddy scramble to get into his overalls and hurry to the back door. Mr. Watts was so excited he could hardly talk. I heard Daddy say, "What are you doin' with a gun?"

"I'm tryin' to tell you. I was sound asleep and a noise woke me up. I realized there was someone in the house."

Daddy unlatched the screen door and stepped outside. I sneaked to the bedroom door. I heard Mr. Watts say, "I always keep a loaded gun by the bed. The burglar didn't hear me when I got up. I took him by surprise and hit him over the head with the butt of the gun. He took off out the back door, leavin' a trail a blood behind him."

He didn't think it was anyone from the camp, because the man took off, leaving his car parked with the motor running, just outside our window. Mr. Watts and Daddy went outside and I went into the living room with Mama and we both lay down on a bed by the window. She started talking to Mrs. Watts through the screen. Mama said, "Why'd he leave his car?"

Mrs. Watts said, "He was too scared to stop. He knowed Lester was on his heels. Why on earth he picked our old house I don't know. We ain't got nothin' worth stealin', let alone worth riskin' your life for."

The front door slammed. Robert and Sid joined Daddy and the Wattses in the space between the houses. Sid asked why the motor was running.

"Get away from that car," Daddy said. "It ain't a toy. You boys stay here. We're goin' down the road to call the police."

Daddy and Mr. Watts walked down the street and used the phone outside the market. In a few minutes I heard sirens, and soon, red lights were flashing all over. Two policemen shined flashlights inside the car and checked it out. One of them reached in and turned the motor off. They questioned Mr. Watts and Daddy, standing in the yard. Had they ever seen the car before? Did they have any idea who owned it? Had the burglar taken anything? Was anything missing?

Mrs. Watts said she thought she had heard the back door open. "But it wasn't until I heard him stumble over a empty bucket settin' against the wall in the kitchen that I knowed someone was in the house." And no, she didn't think anything was missing, because the burglar didn't have time to take anything.

Mr. Watts said, "Wherever he's at, he's got a headache. I split his head open with the butt a my gun, and he's bleedin'."

Lying across the bed next to Mama with my face in the window, I could have reached out and touched that old car. I heard everything that went on. The police circled through the camp with their searchlight. The lights were out in all the cabins. Only the Wattses and the Grants were aware of the cause of the excitement. Finally the police left and drove out Dairy Avenue. In a little while, they were back.

They had found a light on in the camp about a mile away, and inside the cabin, they found a man with his head split open. His friends were trying to bandage him up. He was in the backseat of the police car, and they were taking him by the hospital and then to jail.

The next morning, the scary old car was still by our house, like it was haunting us. Sometime in the afternoon it just disappeared.

The burglary was the talk of the camp. Mama had her own opinion. She said, "Now maybe you girls will understand why Daddy is so strict. I heard someone say that man probably got the wrong house. Said he was most likely lookin' for the house with all the girls."

That made us reflect a bit. We told Mama about one night several months before when a man walked up to our bedroom window as we got ready for bed. We had heard someone walking on the road. The footsteps came closer, and the next thing we knew there he was standing with his face against the screen. He had looked right in at us. We were half-dressed, and I leaped onto one of the beds, grabbed for the light switch, lost my balance, and hit the wall. I reached for it again and there was Tink right beside me, reaching and pulling.

We laughed and told Mama how our hands got tangled in the light cord, and then we lost it. We had grabbed onto it again as the four little girls started laughing. In the midst of the scrambling one of us, or maybe both, yanked hard and turned the light off. But our hands were still tangled and a second later the light was back on, then off, then back on. Finally the scramble ended and the room went dark. The man in the window staggered back onto the street. When we told Mama that story, she told us to remember we weren't living out in the country anymore. And it did cause us to be more careful.

After that I took comfort in the fact that Robert and Sid slept on the front porch and that both doors were bolted.

His Name Was David

ONE SATURDAY MORNING a noisy old flatbed truck drove into the field with two little kids riding on the back. They parked at the end of our rows. The kids jumped off into the dirt as a young man wearing a floppy straw hat and overalls got out carrying a toddler in his arms. The mother slid out the other side and laid a baby on the seat. She was very thin, and the well-worn dress she had on hung like a sack on her tall frame. The little boy, about four years old, stumbled along through the field with his parents while the girl was left to care for the toddler and baby.

The first time they went by, Mama said, "Daddy, did you see that little boy's eyes? Looks like he can't hardly see." We could see his eyes were almost glued shut from infection. He kept rubbing them and whining. He couldn't keep up with his parents, and his mother sent him back to the truck.

"I know," Daddy said. "Seems like they could get somethin' at the drugstore to clear that up. Looks awful, but maybe they ain't got the money. And sometimes a person's just too backward and scared to ask for help."

The baby cried and the little girl tried to feed him, but he wouldn't take the bottle. After a while, it fell in the dirt and she left it there. At lunchtime the mother breast-fed the baby while they all sat on the ground and ate from one can of pork and beans. Then the young couple returned to the field. Mama couldn't stand it. She said to us, "I'm gonna take them little kids some cupcakes." We each had a package of two. We opened them, took one, and gave the others to her.

When the kids saw those chocolate cakes, their eyes lit up. The little girl stood and grabbed them from Mama's hand and passed them to the other kids. Mama checked on the baby who was asleep on the seat of the truck.

A few days later, Bill Dethro came for Daddy to drive a mechanical picker, and we kids were back in school. Mama came home in the evening with stories about the family. Sometimes she was so sad she couldn't eat supper. She said, "The baby cries all day and the little girl tries to feed him from a dirty bottle. The only time he stops crying is at lunch, when the woman feeds him. And the boy's sore eyes are getting worse." Talking about it made Mama cry.

Daddy said, "I know, Mama, I've seen them. They're a pitiful sight. But you can't help them by not eatin'. There ought to be a way folks like that can get help."

Mama went on grieving over those children, until one Sunday morning when our pastor, Brother Jefferson, announced that a four-year-old boy from one of the labor camps had died from what the paper called malnutrition. He asked us to pray for the family. Mama looked at Daddy as if to say, "I knew this would happen." Deep down, I knew who it was.

After church, Sister Jefferson followed our family outside and asked if Tink, Louise, and I would sing at the funeral. Mama asked which camp the family was from. Sister Jefferson said they'd been living in Fred Roby's camp in a tent, sleeping on dirt floors and covering with cotton sacks.

At noon the next day, Tink and I left school to go to the funeral. I felt sick as we practiced "Will the Circle Be Unbroken." Shortly before two, we drove a couple miles out of town to a cemetery with a small chapel. Sister Jefferson gave us last-minute instructions and told us where to sit. At the front of the chapel was a small open coffin, beautifully lined with white satin. We could see the form of a child's head lying on a satin pillow. Three women from church entered and seated themselves near the back.

The organ played "Nearer My God to Thee," and my stomach was tied in knots. I tried to fight my tears, but it was no use. I didn't have a handkerchief and I had to wipe my eyes with the back of my hands, and rub my drippy nose on my arm. I was sixteen years old. My only other experience with funerals was at age three, when Grandma Bristol had carried me in her arms past a coffin with a dead man in it. It was a vague memory.

Sister Jefferson opened with prayer. Tink, Louise, and I stood facing the mostly empty benches. I kept my eyes on the songbook and never looked up. As we began singing "An Unclouded Day," I heard someone almost wailing behind the curtain in the back.

Sister Jefferson didn't change her message a bit that day. She warned the grieving family to get their hearts right with God if they wanted to see "little David" again someday. Her words failed to comfort me.

After the message, we sang a closing song. I had pulled myself together enough to stop crying. The people in attendance filed past and we followed.

My eyes caught sight of the tiny pale corpse in the coffin, and I had to clasp my hands over my mouth and nose to muffle my groan. It came from deep in my gut. I hurried out, with Tink and Louise behind me. We embraced one another, and everyone stood silently as we waited along the walk.

The day was warm, and the door to the chapel stood open. The family was escorted from behind the curtain by the woman who operated the funeral home. They walked to the front to say goodbye to their small son.

Sister Jefferson motioned to us and whispered that they didn't have any pallbearers. She asked us to help her carry the coffin.

Someone had closed it, and the four of us picked it up and carried it down the aisle and through the door. The family and others followed behind into the cemetery and stood beside an open grave. The lady from the funeral home placed a spray of red and white carnations on top of the casket. Sister Jefferson read another scripture: "The Lord giveth, and the Lord taketh away." Then she said a final prayer. At last the funeral was over.

Beneath a tall eucalyptus tree was the flatbed truck. The young father, dressed in overalls, lifted his six-year-old daughter into the cab and helped the toddler in beside her. The mother hugged her baby to her breast, and they went away in the rickety truck.

The family must have moved on. We never saw them again. As Sister Jefferson drove away from the cemetery ground, I looked back at the small coffin with its colorful spray of flowers on the ground beside the open grave, and I said a final good-bye to my childhood.

Commencement

DURING MY CHILDHOOD, a sore throat and swollen tonsils were just part of the cold winter months. The glands in my neck swelled and throbbed. Mama got disturbed at the first sign of a high fever, pressing her hand against my forehead, saying, "Oh my goodness, you're burning up." She bathed me with a cool washcloth to bring the fever down and kept me home from school. She fed me aspirin and made me gargle with warm salt water. I often heard her say to Daddy that they should have my tonsils taken out, that I went through this every winter, but I always bounced back, and the talk of a tonsillectomy somehow got dropped.

The year I was a high school senior, the winter was cold and damp and I had an especially bad bout of swollen glands in my neck. They seemed to throb with every beat of my pulse. I coughed so hard and so much, I tore the raw lining of my throat. I drew comfort from Mama when she washed my face and arms with a cold cloth.

Then, in the night, I woke with the taste of blood in my mouth and a soaked smelly circle on my pillow. I tiptoed into the kitchen and found an empty three-pound coffee can from the trash. I felt around in the dark and found a dishtowel on the cabinet top, and made it back to bed without waking any of the others.

I put the can on the floor, turned my pillow over, placed the towel under my face, and lay on the very edge of the bed. I was all rigged up so that I could sleep. I dozed off.

Later, I woke up feeling sick to my stomach. This time, I was sure that as I coughed, chunks of flesh broke loose from my throat, and a lot of blood went into the can. My stomach turned at the slaughterhouse smell rising from the container. Each time I gagged or coughed, the bleeding worsened. Finally I calmed down, covered the coffee can with my towel, and fell asleep again.

I woke up vomiting blood. The next thing I knew, Mama was standing over me screaming, "Betty! Betty! Can you hear me? Honey, wake up!" She lifted the towel from the can. "What happened, baby? Why didn't you wake me?"

I was groggy, and my throat felt as if it would rip apart if I talked, but I tried to tell her that it had been bleeding and now it was better. I kept my head on the pillow, wishing she would cover me and leave me alone.

She steered me into the living room and put me to bed on the couch. The next thing I knew I was rinsing my mouth out with warm salt water. She pressed my tongue down with a spoon handle and looked into my swollen throat. "It's almost stopped," she said. "Your face is still warm, but not like yesterday." She was crying as she said, "You could a bled to death. Why didn't you wake me!"

I was too weak to move. She spoon-fed me chips of ice, and bombarded me with questions about what had passed in the night. While I slept, Jimmy and Kitty played on the living room floor. After a few hours, I was hungry, and their graham crackers looked good, but I knew my throat was too raw. I didn't dare try to eat.

That afternoon, Aunt Ida walked across the field to our house. Through tears, Mama told her what happened. "How could it happen?" she said, describing the coffee can, the soaked pillow. "And me not know! She could've died in the night, and we would've slept right through it."

They stood over me and I felt as if the whole world was focused on me. "Do you reckon she should be took to the doctor?" Aunt Ida asked. "She's awful pale."

Mama said I looked better. "I'll wait 'til Bill gets home, and we'll see what he says. I'm afraid to give her anything but ice. I'm afraid she'll start bleedin' again."

When Daddy got home from plowing stalks under, I was showered with attention again. Mama had cleaned up the mess, though, and no one but the two of us seemed to realize just what had happened. Daddy walked to the store for a half-gallon tub of vanilla ice cream. I was starved and I enjoyed the rare treat with my brothers and sisters. Even Mama and Daddy had some.

That night, I slept on the couch only a few feet from my parents. My fever was gone. My stomach settled. In a few days, my throat stopped hurting. I was caught up in the excitement of my senior year. I never suffered from tonsillitis again.

Two weeks before graduation, my classmates boarded the school bus for a week-long trip to Canada. They took sleeping bags, with plans to stay in gyms along the way. I felt cheated through all the bake sales and car washes that raised money for the trip, but I assumed that Daddy would say no, so I never asked. On the Saturday that my class pulled out of town, I thinned cotton to earn money for a new outfit to wear for baccalaureate and graduation.

The long hallway seemed deserted on Monday morning as I worked the combination to my locker, tucked my books away, and headed for P.E., but I soon realized I was not the only one who stayed home. There were a half dozen of us. Mr. Douglas put me to work grading papers to help pass the long boring week.

The next thing I knew, the other students had returned and we were practicing for commencement. We gathered outside the auditorium to wait for the principal, Mr. Adams, to place us in alphabetical order. I was chatting with Hazel Thomas. She was my first black classmate. We had met in Mr. Walker's English class my first day at Corcoran High School, and she was one of the few kids I ever got acquainted with who wasn't from the labor camps like me. I knew she was a good student because we checked one another's papers.

The mood was a little silly that day, so I was stunned when she said, "I don't know why I'm bothering to go through with this. It don't mean nothin'."

"It's graduation! We're gonna get our high school diploma. That's excitin' to me!" I said.

Hazel said, "I can't get a job. No one will hire me. You can go to work in a store or office. Even the bank. You see any colored people working in them places? They won't even take my application. All I can do is pick cotton or clean houses. I got no need for a diploma."

"But I pick cotton, too, Hazel."

"Yes, but I saw you wrappin' presents at the Mercantile at Christmas. You think they'd hire me to do that?"

There was a sad ring of truth to her words, but I didn't really understand. After twelve years of school, I didn't know anything about the history of black people. I knew about famous explorers, from Marco Polo to Colombus. I had studied Oklahoma history and had experienced bad dreams over the savagery of brutal Indians murdering white women and children. I'd made an A in American History, learning the names of every U.S. President from George Washington to Harry Truman. I could recite the Gettysburg Address. But I had no idea what the Civil War was about. I hadn't learned anything about slavery. I couldn't understand why my nice, smart, deserving friend Hazel would be denied a good job.

That night I asked my parents about it. Daddy said Hazel was right. He said it was wrong, but that was how it was. "Fred Roby's the only farmer around here that'll hire a colored man to drive a tractor. Guys in the field call him 'Old Nigger Lover.'"

Mama said it was too bad, but we couldn't do anything about it, and it wasn't easy for white people, either.

Then Daddy said, "You girls ain't got no business worryin' about gettin' a job. I don't like seein' women workin' out in public. One of these days you'll be gettin' married, and a woman's place is at home."

Yet he was insistent that we finish high school. I knew my future would be an uphill battle with him, but I tried not to think about that. I wanted to think about graduating.

That night, the band played "Pomp and Circumstance," and Hazel and I took our places in line, wearing caps and gowns, and we marched down the long aisle in the auditorium. Each of us did the exact same thing: we walked across the stage, received our diplomas, and shook hands with Gerald Schwank, president of the school board. Then we said our good-byes.

After that night, I never saw Hazel again. She lived across the tracks, and there was no reason for our paths to cross.

ॐ

The week after graduation I was back in the field, and I spent the summer thinning and weeding cotton. Then my cousin Lorene got me a job with her, working in the scale house at J.G. Boswell's cotton gin. It was a fun job. The trucks would pull in and park just beyond the scales, leaving only the trailer packed with cotton sitting on the scales. Each trailer had a number like 1027 or 1033. I wrote the number of the trailer on a worksheet, along with the gross number of pounds, and kept the worksheets in a tray in front of me. When the same trailer came back through, I recorded the tare weight of the empty trailer on the same worksheet underneath the gross number of pounds and put that one in a separate pile. The worksheet was then ready to be picked up by a coworker who subtracted the tare weight from the gross number of pounds, and that told us how many pounds of cotton had been taken into the gin. When we finished, the worksheets were all sent to the main headquarters in Los Angeles. They had a record of all the cotton that had been picked and taken into the Corcoran gin. Our boss's name was Rudy. He and the scale house crew were all fun to work with. But that job only lasted three and a half months before I was back in the fields again.

At age twenty-two I got a job at Carl's Market on Dairy Avenue, which eventually led to my joining the Retail Clerks Union.

Armageddon

LESS THAN A MONTH after my class graduated, Communist-ruled North Korea invaded South Korea in an effort to unite the country. The United States rushed thousands of troops and huge supplies of equipment to aid South Korea. With World War II hardly behind us, my classmates were suddenly facing the draft again for a "police action" that would scatter them across the globe. Many boys who were not enrolled in college enlisted. Others were drafted. Before long, boys were coming home in body bags.

Sister Jefferson had powerful new fuel for her preaching. "It's Armageddon!" she cried. "The rivers are flowin' with blood. And the Beast, Communism, is setting the stage to take over the world. Christians will be forced to receive the mark and swear allegiance to the Beast. If you don't, you can neither buy nor sell, but anyone who takes the mark will be doomed for eternity to the fires of hell. Take on the armor of God. We must be prepared to die for our Christian faith!"

One day I asked her, "Why did God put us here?"

She said, "To get us ready for heaven."

I knew she meant well, but that didn't make sense. She helped the poor and visited the sick. She cared about hungry children. But I didn't think she knew what she was talking about when she shouted about Armageddon, about hell, and the Beast. If I had little kids, I thought, I would never expose them to this kind of talk.

I told Tink, "I wish she would get a new sermon."

Tink said, "But what if they do try to make us take the mark of the Beast? Would you? Don't that scare you? Sometimes I'm afraid to go to sleep at night, thinkin' I might die and go to hell."

I tried to be brave. I didn't think Sister Jefferson was right about the Book of Revelations, but some of the things I heard about Communism made my blood run cold.

She preached every Sunday morning. Sunday night, it was Brother Jefferson's turn. He waved his arms and jumped and yelled. The world was coming to an end and he would be among the few who were saved. "Saved!" he shouted. Me, I didn't want the world to end, not even to be saved. I wanted to live.

Brother Jefferson told us stories of torture and suffering. Woe unto anyone who wasn't strong enough to die for the cause of Christ. I tried to believe his talk didn't disturb me, but somewhere, deep inside, it did.

Ŋ

One night I dreamed I was hiding on the edge of a wooded area, watching a group of men drag another man into a clearing. They tied him to stake. The man struggled to free himself while the other men piled sticks and tree limbs at his feet. He tugged at the ropes that bound him as the wood at his feet grew higher. I lay with my belly on the ground, peeking through the trees. One of the men lit a torch and threw it into the pile of brush. The flames climbed upward, and I could hardly see the prisoner for the plumes of smoke. He never cried out, though he struggled.

Then he coughed and for just a moment I got a glimpse of his face. I jumped and ran, screaming, "Dad-d-d-d-y!" Then I woke up crying. My heart was broken. It had been so very real. I lay in the dark bedroom, feeling completely alone. Judy stirred beside me, turned over, and pulled the covers up to her face, then fell back into a deep sleep, undisturbed.

The next morning when Mama woke me, I cried and told her I

saw Daddy burned at the stake because of his religious beliefs. She tried to comfort me.

"Honey, I know how real dreams can seem. They can break your heart, but it was only a dream." Then she sent me to wake the other kids. She said if I got busy, the hurt would go away.

As I ate breakfast, it was hard for me to picture Daddy at that moment bouncing along on a tractor somewhere out in the lake basin, but I tried, and as the day wore on, the dream did grow dimmer. From time to time, though, I could still see his face through the smoke and flames.

That evening, he took me aside. "Mama told me about your dream. Baby, you can't believe everything Brother Jefferson says. From now on you just go to church and play your guitar and sing. Don't pay no attention to Brother Jefferson. He just likes to hear his head rattle."

I wanted to say, "But, Daddy, why do we have to go there? Why can't we go to Assembly of God with Aunt Addie?" But I had learned long ago not to question him.

He picked up my guitar from the bed, lifted his eyebrows, smiled his mischievous smile, and said, "Here, play me a song."

I wanted to say, "I don't feel like it now," but I managed a half smile and strummed and hummed, trying to remember something from my instruction book. Finally I took off on "You Are My Sunshine." I knew if I managed it right, I could stay away from anything that reminded me of Brother Jefferson.

෴

A tall black stranger came to church one night and shifted the whole atmosphere of Brother Jefferson's congregation. He stepped into a pew near the back and raised his arms upward. His melodious voice rang out above the others as we sang, "When the Saints Go Marching In."

There was something about his deep voice that produced a soothing calmness. I closed my eyes, and my hands worked a perfect harmony on the guitar. By the end of the song, this charismatic man was in the aisle, clapping his hands and marching in perfect time to the music. Sister Lillie Mae stepped in behind him, copying his steps as she followed. A few others joined them. Brother and Sister Jefferson left the platform and entered the march. He never slowed up, but glided around and started another circle around the church.

To my surprise, Daddy stepped into the aisle, too. Tears were rolling down his cheeks as he sang and clapped his hands, falling into line behind the marchers. Then the choir left the stage and joined in. By now almost everyone was in the line that kept circling, singing, clapping hands, and circling again. It must have lasted for fifteen minutes. All the while, my friends Robert and Jesse and I played our guitars. I felt I was contributing to an atmosphere of love.

People made their way back to their pews. Brother Jefferson escorted the charismatic stranger onto the platform. His hand rested on the man's shoulder as they stood behind the pulpit. He took the man's hand and lifted their arms into the air and said, "Brothers and Sisters, this is my good friend, the Reverend Brother Griggs."

Brother Griggs shouted, "Praise God! Hallelujah!" He raised his other arm into the air and danced a jig as shouts went up from the crowd. Brother Jefferson tried to mimic his steps, but he just didn't have it.

Brother Jefferson explained that the two of them had been pastors in the town of Tipton and that their congregations had worshiped together many times. Brother Griggs was pastor of Orange Avenue Holy Ghost Tabernacle on the north side of Corcoran.

Brother Jefferson asked Brother Griggs to testify. Again there was leaping and dancing and swaying. Sister Lillie Mae jumped into the aisle and danced, and the walls vibrated with the cries of *Amen!* And *Hallelujah!* And *Praise the Lord!*

Brother Jefferson invited Brother Griggs and his congregation to join us in a revival meeting the following Sunday. The display that night was only a preview of what was to come. Services started at seven o'clock in the evening and lasted until eleven and sometimes midnight. Brother Griggs's son, James, played a mean piano. He played old gospel songs like they were jazz. The black congregation would take one line of a song, such as "I know the Lord has laid His hand on me," and repeat it many times until the aisles were filled with dancing and the roof seemed likely to lift off the church.

Then one of their members stood to give a testimony, more often than not dancing herself into a trance while the others sang. Again, others joined, singing and dancing. The services were a celebration, with music, singing, shouting, and dancing. It was a grand old time.

The word got out after the first meeting, and people who rarely went to church came, brought their families, and packed the house. Most stayed until services ended. Daddy, though, motioned to me and Tink after a couple of hours and said, "Let's go." He loved the revival, but five o'clock in the morning came early and he was thinking of us going to school.

Once in a while, we visited Brother Griggs's church. They celebrated life there, and they enriched ours. Their way of worshiping made me forget all about Armageddon.

A Record

JOYCE CRAWFORD, the girl I met my very first day at Corcoran High School, was my friend all through high school. We attended the same church and picked cotton together. Every fall her dad, Bub, ran a crew of pickers for one of the small farmers.

One day, Joyce and I decided to set a record for ourselves. Our goal was to pick three hundred pounds before quitting time. We also raced to see who would reach it first. We stayed within a few pounds of one another all day.

Because her dad was boss, she couldn't go home until the last person left the field. That day, he stayed with Joyce and me until sunset, though he usually quit before then. When we weighed our last load, we were both short of our goal by four or five pounds.

"We need to go back," we said.

"Ah, come on, girls," Bub said. "Finish it out in the morning."

"That ain't pickin' three hundred in a day," I said.

Daddy laughed. "They got you there, Bub. If they're gonna pick three hundred pounds in one day, they ain't done it yet."

"We won't take long," I said. "We'll pick real fast. You'll stay, won't you, Daddy?"

"If Bub'll wait, I will. But don't be too long, it'll start to get dark pretty soon."

Joyce and I returned to the field all alone. The sun sank behind the horizon as we stuffed big handfuls of cotton into our sacks, setting a record for ourselves. Daddy emptied our sacks while Bub loaded his scales and prepared to leave the field. At dusk we drove from the field. I flashed a proud smile at Joyce as she climbed into the cab of their pickup with her dad. Now we could both boast that we had picked three hundred pounds of cotton in one day. It was the only time either of us did it.

Ignited Fumes

DADDY WAS A DEPENDABLE, capable worker, so foreman Bill Dethro kept him working almost year-round. Daddy went from plowing with a team of horses to working with complicated machinery. One of his favorite jobs was driving a weed burner, or sprayer, keeping the irrigation ditch banks clean.

A large tank filled with fuel was mounted on a truck, with a boom extending about twenty feet. One man drove and another operated the boom, spraying the weeds. Fuel trucks drove into the fields to supply the weed burner and other equipment with fuel.

One day, Daddy and his coworker discovered a leak in the tank of the weed burner. It was nearly five in the afternoon when they ran out of fuel and drove into Uncle Clinton's shop for repair. Uncle Clinton worked an eight-hour day as a welder. It was Friday and almost time to go home for the weekend. When Uncle Clinton picked up his torch and goggles, Daddy asked him, "Ain't you gonna fill that tank with water?"

Uncle Clinton said, "Aw, it's just a tiny speck of a leak. We'll have it done in two seconds."

"But it's full of fumes," Daddy said. "They always fill it with water before they do any weldin'."

"Bill, do you know how long it'll take to run that thing full of water? Look at the clock. It's quittin' time. I can't hardly see the leak. You step back, I'll have this thing fixed up in no time."

Uncle Clinton and his coworker climbed onto the tank as Daddy and his coworker walked toward the door. The second the torch was lit, it ignited the fumes. The tank exploded, throwing all four men across the shop. One man sailed through the open doors. Daddy landed against the wall. When he tried to get up, he discovered that his right ankle was broken. Uncle Clinton and the other welder lay on the ground a few yards away. Daddy said, "Their hair was singed and their faces burned 'til I couldn't tell who was who. I thought they was dead."

Workers from the yard rushed in, and a few minutes later, sirens were heard all over town as the ambulance and fire trucks rushed out Whitley Avenue to haul four charred men to Corcoran Hospital.

Mama and I went to the hospital room where Daddy was. Despite his blackened hair and face, his smile was unmistakable. His leg was elevated in a cast. I didn't recognize anyone else until I heard Uncle Clinton's hearty laugh. Underneath the oozing splotches and medication on his face and hands, his flesh was charred.

Daddy was released the next morning. Laid up with a broken ankle, he was unable to work for six weeks. One day he said, "Get me a hammer, Mama. I ain't wearin' this cast no longer."

"You can't break that cast off," Mama said. "Dr. Jacob will take it off when he releases you for work."

"Who says I can't?" Daddy hobbled toward the porch.

"If you bust it off yourself, you'll be stuck with the bill. You're covered with insurance on the job, but if you go back to work before the doctor says it's OK, they might not pay it."

"Who's gonna tell them? Huh? They'll never know. I'm tired of settin' here. I need to go to work."

He broke the cast off. Robert was irrigating nights. Daddy said, "Son, see if you can get me a job with you." The next evening, he was in the field shoveling dirt, releasing water from one row to another and damming up spots where water was getting away.

When he returned to Dr. Jacob's office for his next appointment, Daddy told us, "Dr. Jacob laughed and said, 'Bill, you're one of a kind. There's not another person in the world who'd do that.'" The insurance company paid the bills and he never heard a word about removing the cast himself.

Uncle Clinton returned to his welding job. The top layer of flesh on his face has been singed off, but the burns weren't deep. He healed with very little scarring.

༉

For several weeks, Daddy and Robert irrigated Salyer Land Company's home ranch east of Corcoran. One night, in the wee hours of the morning, they witnessed a strange flash of green light in the eastern sky. Daddy described it like this: "The atmosphere lit up from one horizon to the other. For a few seconds, a green dome covered the earth. It was light as day. Then it disappeared."

That spring, the hydrogen bomb was being tested in the Nevada desert.

"Seems Like We're Home"

WE STARTED PICKING SEASON again in Bub Crawford's crew. One day I was in line near the cotton trailer, waiting for my sixty-seven pounds to be emptied, when Bub asked Daddy, "Bill, do you ever think about goin' back home?"

"No, not anymore," Daddy said. "I had a hard time settlin' myself when we first got here. I was determined to go back and try to get a little farm of my own. But now it don't make no sense to leave. Robert's married and we got a grandbaby. Betty's out of high school. Like Elsie says, 'Seems like we're home.'"

Bub said he was going to take his family and go back to McAllister, Oklahoma. He thought maybe Daddy would like to buy his house.

At first Daddy said he didn't see how he could. But Bub kept talking. Our rent was thirty-five dollars a month, and Bub's house payments were only forty-five. The house was solid, built by Bub's brother-in-law on fifteen acres of land, with a good well, and the water was piped in. There were three bedrooms. There was still work to do on the bathroom, and there wasn't a hot water heater, but it would be a wonderful improvement on Dairy Avenue.

"It sounds pretty good," Daddy said, "but what about a down payment?"

"I thought about that," Bub said. "I need a truck. Give me that half-ton pickup of yours, take over my payments, and we got a deal."

I held my breath until I heard Daddy say, "I'll bring Elsie over this evenin' and take a look. How's that?"

"I'll be lookin' for you.

⌁

And just that fast, Daddy bought a house. Bub's mortgage was four thousand dollars, payable at forty-five dollars a month. After four years on Dairy Avenue, we packed up and left the labor camp behind.

The house had never had a coat of paint. Daddy and Robert painted it white with a dark green trim. Tink and I walked a mile and a half into Main Street and bought curtains at Sprouse Reitze five and dime store. We laughed and clowned as we hung the ninety-eight-cent flowered plastic curtains in the windows. I felt as if we were decorating a mansion.

The winter fog moved in about the same time we did. From the front door, I could barely see across the road. Beyond the open field, through the soupy gray mist, traffic on Dairy Avenue passed, sending its sounds up to us.

One afternoon, I heard the heavy yellow school bus sway side to side as it rounded the corner, grinding to a stop. I smiled, hearing the cheerful voices of school kids scattering in every direction. "Hey, everybody! Race you home," Sid yelled.

The bus roared past our house. Five pairs of feet pounded the pavement as my laughing siblings came into sight through a curtain of fog. Our family had taken root. We were home.

Another Long Journey

IN THE EARLY SIXTIES, mechanical pickers were slowly taking over the cotton fields. Daddy drove a cotton picker, but Mama still weeded cotton in the summer and worked wherever hand-picking could be found in the fall.

At that time, my job with the Retail Clerks Union—medical and other benefits not included—paid more than twice as much as Daddy's wages from driving farm equipment. I worked in an air-conditioned building while Mama was stuck in the penetrating heat of the fields for seventy-five cents an hour. My heart ached at the thought of her and my siblings still working in the fields.

Among the laborers in California's San Joaquin Valley was a thirty-year-old man by the name of Cesar Chavez. His parents lost their home in Arizona during the Depression and were forced to work as migrants. Cesar Chavez had felt all the indignities of the treatment of farm workers since he was ten years old. He walked out of the fields and raised his voice in protest. He began his lifelong work of bringing farm laborers' faces and their stories to the American public. His aim was to help them achieve a livable wage. More than that, he knew they deserved to be treated with dignity and respect. Organizing had been tried before. Farm workers gave their lives trying it. But Chavez believed the time had come, and his first task was to organize a union.

"This will be a long journey," Chavez said. "Some of us will be the bridges and others the posts, others will be the roads, and everyone will pass over us." Knowing there was a lot of hard work ahead of them, he told the workers, "Yeah, we're gonna pray a little and we're gonna work a lot."

About a year after they began organizing, grape pickers in Delano, California, walked out of the vineyards. Night after night, the workers were shown carrying picket signs. Soon the strike brought together all workers—Mexicans, Filipinos, blacks, and whites—who had for years been kept apart by racial barriers. The strike united them all.

Chavez's struggle had begun in the grape vineyards at Delano, but it was felt in the cotton fields of the Tulare Lake Basin, the lettuce fields in the Salinas Valley, and as far away as the tomato fields in Iowa. Soon he was joined by people of all races, religions, and background.

Walter Ruther, president of the United Auto Workers, came to Delano and carried a sign alongside Cesar Chavez and the grape cutters. He pledged five thousand dollars a month to the United Farm Workers for as long as it took them to win their struggle with the growers.

Robert Kennedy paid a visit to California in support of Chavez and the farm workers. The two men embraced. They attended mass together. Kennedy walked among the people, shaking hands. And in a speech he said, "Make no mistake about it, decency is at the heart of the matter, and poverty is indecent. We can do much better than we have done in the past."

The grape boycott was national news. It became an international affair. Growers felt pressure abroad as well as at home. Stores couldn't give their grapes away. They tried to give grapes with every ten-dollar grocery order, but people refused to take the grapes home.

Growers had to come to terms with the union if they wanted to continue the grape industry. After a few weeks of peaceful negotiations, growers in Delano signed contracts with the United Farm Workers' Union.

The first battle was over. The contract brought decent wages, along with little things like cool water. I couldn't believe it when I saw portable toilets in the fields.

Daddy's wages went up and Mama, in her early fifties, was able to stay home. Long before his retirement, Daddy drove an air-conditioned tractor, and the mechanical cotton pickers were equipped with heaters for the cold December months.

Chavez's fight for fairness and decency continued until his death in Mesa, Arizona, in 1993, where he had gone to defend a law suit against the United Farm Workers' Union. He was sixty-two.

Several thousand hardworking people of all races joined Chavez in his final march. Celebrities like the Kennedys and Jesse Jackson took turns carrying his body as it rested in a pine box his brother had made.

Paying tribute to Cesar Chavez would require another book, and any effort on my part is clumsy and inadequate at best. But of one thing I am certain: while the life of a farm worker is never easy, it's a lot better today, thanks to the dedication of Cesar Chavez and the United Farm Workers' Union.

An Afterwards

DADDY WAS A FARMER. He didn't know anything else and didn't want to be anything else. If his sisters hadn't been living in the farming area of California's San Joaquin Valley, I doubt if they could have ever lured him away from his roots in Oklahoma.

He had never driven a tractor before he went to California. Grandpa Gore had owned a tractor, but Daddy never touched it. He always owned a good team of work horses, and my childhood was spent trailing barefoot behind him in the freshly plowed ground. There was a feeling of ecstasy out there with the cool damp earth beneath my feet. And maybe that is why I always understood when he turned down jobs in Boswell's cotton gin and other jobs inside the shops where he could have worked without having to fight the elements. Daddy said there was a feeling of freedom in the wide-open spaces that could not be found anyplace else. And he loved to plow and plant and watch things grow.

Things changed fast after World War II. I'm sure my Daddy had no idea how fast he would have to make adjustments to a whole new way of life. He was driving a tractor in a matter of months after we arrived in California, and that same year, the first mechanical cotton picker was introduced to the Tulare Lake Basin.

True to himself, Daddy remained a farm laborer. He plowed the land, and he planted. Irrigation water came down from the Sierra Nevada through the rivers and emptied into the lake basin, and Daddy helped divert it into the fields. He thinned and weeded cotton with a hoe. He burned weeds off ditch banks. And each fall found him behind the wheel of a mechanical cotton picker.

One day, years after I had picked my last row of cotton, Daddy took me into the lake basin and showed me a square-mile section of sunflowers in full bloom. What a beautiful sight it was. Other crops were introduced to the area, and he knew each new crop and what it was for. Safflowers, for instance, was a completely new word to him, but not for long.

After retirement, he returned to the field and worked through picking season and earned as much money as the government would allow. By then he said he could pick the season when he wanted to work. When he retired, a picture of him driving the Tulare Lake Basin's first two-row cotton picker decorated one wall of a local bank. At present, it is with the Corcoran Chamber of Commerce. He spoke of Oklahoma from time to time, but he learn to love the California sunshine and never saw his beloved Oklahoma again.

In October 2003 Mama and Daddy celebrated their seventy-fifth wedding anniversary in their own home. Daddy died in June 2004. He was ninety-eight years old.

At this writing, Mama is ninety-five and still with us.

Grandma Bristol died in Antioch, California, in 1990. She was 107.

⁂

More than fifty years have passed since my parents bought the house on Vandorsten Avenue on the south edge of Corcoran, California. Though we children have all moved on, there remains a bond among us that only siblings can know. Even death cannot break it.

Of our three brothers, Robert, the oldest, worked for a Boise Cascade plywood mill in Oregon until his death from a brain tumor in 1980. Sid is retired from the Plumbers Union; he spent thirty-five years traveling the length and breadth of the San Joaquin Valley as a refrigeration mechanic. Jimmy, our youngest brother, who in 1966 was the last of us to graduate from Corcoran High School, has also been a member of the Plumbers Union for more than thirty years, with two years off during the Vietnam War. He has helped to build everything from hospitals and schools to state prisons all over the state of California.

My five sisters are homemakers. June died in March 1997, after a seventeen-year battle with lupus. I was able to share my writing with her, and I was grateful for her enthusiasm. I regret she could not live to see our family's story in print.

Judy and Tink are mothers and grandmothers. Susie is the only one of the nine children to remain in Corcoran, where her husband, Joe, works for the city. Her love and dedication to the care of our parents is something the rest of us can never repay her for.

Kitty graduated from College of the Sequoias in Visalia, California, in 1967. She married the same year and moved to Oregon. She was involved with schools for many years, and is now active with St. Vincent de Paul Society, where she works with the poor.

I belonged to the Retail Clerks Union for more than twenty years before taking up private nursing duty in a retirement residence. There I met and married Ransom Henshaw when I was fifty-one. At that time, after working hard for many years, I was able to retire. I regret that Ransom did not live to see my story completed.

I never had a child of my own, but there has been a never-ending stream of little children in my life. Just last year a five-year-old said, "What was your favorite TV show when you was a little girl?"

I said, "We didn't have television when I was a little girl."

"You didn't? What did you do?"

"Well, I lived on a farm, and—"

"Did you have animals?"

"Yes."

"Boy!" Quinn said, "I'll bet that was fun!"

Acknowledgments

AS I LOOK BACK over the path my family has traveled—our journey from Oklahoma on Route 66; our life in the labor camp; the awful thirst in the overwhelming heat of the fields; our tired, aching bodies—I have come to look upon that path as a sort of Holy Ground, and I have carried a deep longing to write my memories down. I am forever grateful to all those who helped make this dream come true.

Much thanks to my dear friends Lucia Smith and Lori Tobias, who invited this frightened and inexperienced writer to join their writing group. Over a ten-year period, Lucia has taught me much about writing. She has been my greatest critic and mentor. To my friend Dick Boich, whose editing, honest criticism, and encouragement kept me pressing on. To Marlene King, who not only was helpful as a writing partner but also recruited projects for us in *Writer* magazine. To instructor Sharon Olson, who told me I could write and helped get my first piece published. To Bill Johnson at Willamette Writers in Portland, who not only taught me about writing but also helped me with editing early on. And to my wonderful friend in the Netherlands, Jim Forest, who graciously read my work and whose encouragement was invaluable. We met through Thomas Merton's writing and I was fortunate enough to have met him in Portland in 1996. Peace be with you always, Jim.

And finally, many, many thanks to my friend and editor, Sandra Scofield, without whom *Children of the Dust* would not be where it is today. Sandra recognized my work as something that should be in the hands of a university press and helped send it to TTUP editor Judith Keeling. Sandra has been more than an editor. Her help has been invaluable. Without her I would still be struggling. Much thanks to Judith Keeling, as well, whose enthusiasm helped get this work published.

Thanks to my family members who helped me locate family photos and to my cousin, Dale Beck, for his help on the family tree.

Index

The author and Texas Tech University Press are deeply grateful to The CH Foundation, without whose generous support the book series Plains Histories would not have been possible.

❧